On Earth

3 Christmas Carols
from Around the World

ISBN 0-7935-6679-7

HAL•LEONARD®
CORPORATION
7777 W. BLUEMOUND RD. P.O. BOX 13819 MILWAUKEE, WI 53213

CONTENTS

Austria

10 As Lately We Watched
11 Gloria
12. Silent Night, Holy Night
13 Still, Still, Still

Belgium

14 The Simple Birth

Canada

15 The Huron Carol
16 Whence Art Thou, My Maiden?

Chile

18 Going to Bethlehem

Colombia

17 Quickly Now, O Shepherds

Croatia

20 Hear, O Shepherds

Czech Republic

21 Come, All Ye Shepherds
22 From Out the Deep Woods a Cuckoo Flew
23 I Go to Bethlehem
24 Let Our Gladness Know No End
25 Rocking

Denmark

26 A Child Is Born in Bethlehem
27 Child Jesus
28 Lovely Is the Dark Blue Sky

England

29 As With Gladness Men of Old
30 Away in a Manger
31 The Boar's Head Carol
32 The Cherry Tree Carol
33 Coventry Carol
34 The First Nowell
36 God Rest You Merry, Gentlemen
38 The Golden Carol
39 Good King Wenceslas
40 The Holly and the Ivy
41 I Saw Three Ships
42 In the Bleak Midwinter
43 It Came Upon the Midnight Clear
44 Once in Royal David's City
45 Sussex Carol
46 Wassail Song
47 Wassail, Wassail
48 We Wish You a Merry Christmas
49 What Child Is This?

France

50 Angels We Have Heard on High
51 Bring a Torch, Jeannette, Isabelle
52 He Is Born, the Divine Christ Child
53 Infant So Gentle
54 March of the Three Kings
55 Noël Nouvelet
56 O Come, O Come, Immanuel
58 O Holy Night
57 O Leave Your Sheep
60 Pat-a-pan
61 Shepherd! Shake Off Your Drowsy Sleep
62 The Sleep of the Infant Jesus
64 Touro-Louro-Louro
63 What Is This Fragrance So Appealing?
66 Whence Comes This Rush of Wings Afar?

Germany

67 A Babe Is Born in Bethlehem
68 Beside Thy Cradle Here I Stand
69 Break Forth, O Beauteous Heavenly Light
70 From Heaven Above
71 Good Christian Men, Rejoice (In dulci jubilo)
72 Joseph Dearest, Joseph Mine
73 Lo, How a Rose E'er Blooming
74 O Christmas Tree
75 O Come, Little Children
76 O Thou Joyful
77 Ring, Little Bells
78 Susani
79 To Us Is Born a Little Child
80 While By My Sheep

Ireland

81 Irish Carol
82 Love Came Down at Christmas
83 The Snow Lay on the Ground
84 Wexford Carol

Italy
85 Carol of the Bagpipers
86 From Starry Skies Thou Comest
87 Hark! Ye Shepherds
88 Jesus, the Newborn Baby
89 Mary, Dear Mother of Jesus
90 Oh! Dear Jesus
91 Oh! Infant Jesus
94 Oh! Night Among the Thousands
92 Sleep, O Sleep, My Precious Child

Mexico
95 The Babe
96 Pray, Give Us Lodging

Netherlands
97 In Bethlehem, the Lowly
98 Today We Welcome a Tiny Child

Norway
99 I Am So Glad on Christmas Eve
00 O Christmas, You Season of Childlike Delight
01 You Green and Glittering Tree

Poland
02 Come Running, You Shepherds
03 Infant Holy, Infant Lowly
04 Lullaby, Jesus
05 O Come Rejoicing

Puerto Rico
06 In Bethlehem's Cradle
08 Pastores a Belén
07 Song of the Wise Men

Romania
10 At the Gates of Heaven Above

Scotland
11 Baloo, Lammy

Spain
112 A la nanita nana
113 Bells Over Bethlehem
114 Carol of the Birds
115 Come, All Ye Children
116 Companions All, Sing Loudly
117 A Fire Is Started in Bethlehem
118 Fum, Fum, Fum
119 The Icy December
120 King Herod
121 The Son of Mary
122 Ya viene la vieja

Sweden
123 The Happy Christmas Comes Once More
124 Yuletide Is Here Again

United States of America
125 Away in a Manger
126 Everywhere, Everywhere, Christmas Tonight
127 Gather Around the Christmas Tree
128 Glad Christmas Bells
129 Go, Tell It on the Mountain
130 I Heard the Bells on Christmas Day
131 It Came Upon the Midnight Clear
132 Jingle Bells
133 Jolly Old Saint Nicholas
134 Mary Had a Baby
135 O Little Town of Bethlehem
136 Rise Up Shepherd and Follow
137 There's a Song in the Air
138 Up on the Housetop
139 We Three Kings of Orient Are
140 Winds Through the Olive Trees

Venezuela
141 As the Frightened Baby Jesus
142 We Are Singing

Wales
143 Deck the Hall
144 Welsh Carol

CONTENTS

Alphabetically by carol title.

112	A la nanita nana	Spain
50	Angels We Have Heard on High	France
10	As Lately We Watched	Austria
141	As the Frightened Baby Jesus	Venezuela
29	As With Gladness Men of Old	England
110	At the Gates of Heaven Above	Romania
125	Away in a Manger	United States of America
30	Away in a Manger	England
95	The Babe	Mexico
67	A Babe Is Born in Bethlehem	Germany
111	Baloo, Lammy	Scotland
113	Bells Over Bethlehem	Spain
68	Beside Thy Cradle Here I Stand	Germany
31	The Boar's Head Carol	England
69	Break Forth, O Beauteous Heavenly Light	Germany
51	Bring a Torch, Jeannette, Isabelle	France
85	Carol of the Bagpipers	Italy
114	Carol of the Birds	Spain
32	The Cherry Tree Carol	England
26	A Child Is Born in Bethlehem	Denmark
27	Child Jesus	Denmark
115	Come, All Ye Children	Spain
21	Come, All Ye Shepherds	Czech Republic
102	Come Running, You Shepherds	Poland
116	Companions All, Sing Loudly	Spain
33	Coventry Carol	England
143	Deck the Hall	Wales
126	Everywhere, Everywhere, Christmas Tonight	United States of America
117	A Fire Is Started in Bethlehem	Spain
34	The First Nowell	England
70	From Heaven Above	Germany
22	From Out the Deep Woods a Cuckoo Flew	Czech Republic
86	From Starry Skies Thou Comest	Italy
118	Fum, Fum, Fum	Spain
127	Gather Around the Christmas Tree	United States of America
128	Glad Christmas Bells	United States of America
11	Gloria	Austria
129	Go, Tell It on the Mountain	United States of America
36	God Rest You Merry, Gentlemen	England
18	Going to Bethlehem	Chile
38	The Golden Carol	England
71	Good Christian Men, Rejoice (In dulci jubilo)	Germany
39	Good King Wenceslas	England
123	The Happy Christmas Comes Once More	Sweden
87	Hark! Ye Shepherds	Italy
52	He Is Born, the Divine Christ Child	France
20	Hear, O Shepherds	Croatia
40	The Holly and the Ivy	England
15	The Huron Carol	Canada
99	I Am So Glad on Christmas Eve	Norway
23	I Go to Bethlehem	Czech Republic
130	I Heard the Bells on Christmas Day	United States of America
41	I Saw Three Ships	England
119	The Icy December	Spain
97	In Bethlehem, the Lowly	Netherlands
106	In Bethlehem's Cradle	Puerto Rico
42	In the Bleak Midwinter	England
103	Infant Holy, Infant Lowly	Poland
53	Infant So Gentle	France
81	Irish Carol	Ireland
131	It Came Upon the Midnight Clear	United States of America
43	It Came Upon the Midnight Clear	England
88	Jesus, the Newborn Baby	Italy
132	Jingle Bells	United States of America
133	Jolly Old Saint Nicholas	United States of America
72	Joseph Dearest, Joseph Mine	Germany

20	King Herod	Spain
24	Let Our Gladness Know No End	Czech Republic
73	Lo, How a Rose E'er Blooming	Germany
82	Love Came Down at Christmas	Ireland
28	Lovely Is the Dark Blue Sky	Denmark
04	Lullaby, Jesus	Poland
54	March of the Three Kings	France
89	Mary, Dear Mother of Jesus	Italy
134	Mary Had a Baby	United States of America
55	Noël Nouvelet	France
74	O Christmas Tree	Germany
00	O Christmas, You Season of Childlike Delight	Norway
75	O Come, Little Children	Germany
56	O Come, O Come, Immanuel	France
105	O Come Rejoicing	Poland
58	O Holy Night	France
57	O Leave Your Sheep	France
135	O Little Town of Bethlehem	United States of America
76	O Thou Joyful	Germany
90	Oh! Dear Jesus	Italy
91	Oh! Infant Jesus	Italy
94	Oh! Night Among the Thousands	Italy
44	Once in Royal David's City	England
08	Pastores a Belén	Puerto Rico
60	Pat-a-pan	France
96	Pray, Give Us Lodging	Mexico
17	Quickly Now, O Shepherds	Colombia
77	Ring, Little Bells	Germany
36	Rise Up Shepherd and Follow	United States of America
25	Rocking	Czech Republic
61	Shepherd! Shake Off Your Drowsy Sleep	France
12	Silent Night, Holy Night	Austria
14	The Simple Birth	Belgium
92	Sleep, O Sleep, My Precious Child	Italy
62	The Sleep of the Infant Jesus	France
83	The Snow Lay on the Ground	Ireland
121	The Son of Mary	Spain
107	Song of the Wise Men	Puerto Rico
13	Still, Still, Still	Austria
78	Susani	Germany
45	Sussex Carol	England
137	There's a Song in the Air	United States of America
79	To Us Is Born a Little Child	Germany
98	Today We Welcome a Tiny Child	Netherlands
64	Touro-Louro-Louro	France
138	Up on the Housetop	United States of America
46	Wassail Song	England
47	Wassail, Wassail	England
142	We Are Singing	Venezuela
139	We Three Kings of Orient Are	United States of America
48	We Wish You a Merry Christmas	England
144	Welsh Carol	Wales
84	Wexford Carol	Ireland
49	What Child Is This?	England
63	What Is This Fragrance So Appealing?	France
16	Whence Art Thou, My Maiden?	Canada
66	Whence Comes This Rush of Wings Afar?	France
80	While By My Sheep	Germany
140	Winds Through the Olive Trees	United States of America
122	Ya viene la vieja	Spain
101	You Green and Glittering Tree	Norway
124	Yuletide Is Here Again	Sweden

Christmas Customs Around the World

On December 24, wishes of Merry Christmas ring out throughout the world. The words vary from "Een Plesierige Kerfees" in South Africa to "Nodlaig mhaith chugnat" in Ireland to "God Jul" in Norway to "Sarbatori vesele" in Romania, but the message is the same. For two days out of the year, the entire world pauses to celebrate Christmas with unique customs and observances. Some sing carols or roast a goose. Some create a feast, others prepare plum puddings, while some take swings at piñatas. Music is common to all of these varied Christmas traditions. The familiar carol "Silent Night," for instance, was written in Austria and titled "Stille Nacht." Today it is heard around the world, translated into over ninety languages.

EUROPE

Throughout Europe, Christmas is a time of family gatherings, great music, and enormous feasts. Many of the carols and customs now common around the world have their roots in Europe.

Austria

In Austrian mountain villages, a torch-lit carol singing procession begins Christmas Eve festivities. Starting at the home of the family living the farthest from church, the procession moves from house to house, each family joining in until they all reach the church. In other areas, the Christmas Eve tradition of *Turmmusik* finds brass players taking to the highest point in town and playing chorales as people walk to church. In a tradition called "Showing the Christ-child," families go from home to home carrying a manger and singing carols.

Belgium

Belgian church bells ring as processions of bands, chanting priests, and singing children make their way through the streets on Christmas Eve until they reach the church for midnight services. In Flanders, each church presents an elaborate Christmas play that is a source of great pride and competition between churches. In the small villages of Flanders, three men are appointed to walk through the streets, costumed as the Magi. They stop at each home to sing a song about the journey of the Magi and a Flemish version of "O Tannenbaum."

The Czech Republic

In the Czech Republic, formerly Bohemia, Christmas begins with Svatej Nikulas Day on December 6 and ends on January 6 with the visit of the Tri Kraluy (Three Kings). On December 6, St. Nicholas comes down from the sky, accompanied by an angel and the devil. The angel carries gifts for the good children, and the devil carries switches for the naughty ones. At Christmas dinners, a chair and place setting are always left empty, awaiting the Christ-child.

Denmark

In 1903 a Danish postal clerk named Einar Holboell made Christmas history. It occurred to him that he could raise a fair amount of money for victims of tuberculosis through sales of a special Christmas stamp, intended to be used as an envelope seal on Christmas greeting cards. In the first year he raised some $18,000. The Christmas Seal came to America in 1907 and is now common around the world. The Scandanavian Christmas begins on Saint Lucia's Day, December 13, lasting until Saint Knute's Day, January 13.

France

After midnight worship services, the French begin a feast called *le reveillon*. In Alsace, celebrants dine on goose; in Burgundy, the meal is turkey with chestnuts. The Bretons prepare buckwheat cakes with sour cream, while oysters are served in Paris, where dancing and celebrating continue well into the night. Manger scenes, found in most homes, include the usual figures of Mary, Joseph, the baby Jesus, shepherds, Magi, and cattle, with the additions of policemen, teachers, and other figures from everyday life.

Germany

Germans love their Christmas traditions. Many German homes sport several beautifully decorated Christmas trees as well as the flickering candles of Advent wreaths. The Christmas tree tradition was born in Germany, where, during the Middle Ages, a pine tree was decorated with apples and used as part of a creation ceremony held on December 24. The Christmas tree custom was brought to America by early German settlers.

Looking closely at the Christmas tree of a German household, one is likely to spot a pickle, either real or made of glass, hanging among the decorations. Traditionally, German households did not put up the Christmas tree until Christmas Eve, or in some areas until Christmas Day. The tree would be decorated by the adults, behind closed doors. When it was ready, the doors would be thrown open and the children would rush in to admire the tree and search for the pickle hidden in its branches. The first to find the pickle received a special treat.

Hungary
Christmas in Hungary is a two-day celebration that brings together enormous extended families. Family members gather on Christmas Eve to share a lavish meal and exchange gifts before attending midnight worship services. Children place their shoes or boots under windowsills on Christmas Eve, knowing that their behavior in the last year will bring them either a reward of candies and toys or a shoe full of sticks.

Ireland
Irish families place lit candles in their windows on Christmas Eve as an invitation to all wanderers to come in for a good meal and night's lodging. In the morning, those who have stayed the night are sent on their way with a few coins in their pockets.

Italy
The Italian Christmas holiday is a three-week affair that begins eight days before Christmas with the *novena* and continues until after the Twelfth Night of the Feast of Epiphany. During *novena*, children parade from door to door reciting the Christmas story for a reward of coins. In Italian homes, the *presipio*, a miniature manger scene, is the center of much attention and pride.

After fasting for the twenty-four hours before Christmas, Italians begin their Christmas Eve with as elaborate a banquet as they can afford to create. A cannon fired at sunset from the Castle of St. Angelo in Rome signals the beginning of the holy observance. Churches are filled to the rafters on Christmas Eve as congregations compete to exhibit the grandest *presipio*.

The Netherlands
Christmas begins in the Netherlands on December 6 with the arrival of Saint Nicholas. Accompanied by Black Peter (the devil), Nicholas arrives via boat in every city that has a harbor. He wears a bishop's robe, miter, and white gloves. Thousands flock to the docks, cheering his arrival and forming parades, complete with police motorcades, brass bands, and floats, to lead him to the town square. On Christmas Eve, Christmas Day, and the second Christmas Day (December 26), families and friends gather for worship, dining, and singing.

Norway
As Norwegians feast on *kringle*, *lefse*, and *lutefisk*, the *Julebukk* tradition finds children dressed up in costume going door to door asking for treats. At some point in the Christmas festivities, an adult, dressed as a goat, bursts in and pretends to die and then return to life. This is the last vestige of a pagan ritual practiced by the Vikings but once forbidden by the church. The Scandinavian Christmas begins on Saint Lucia's Day, December 13, lasting until Saint Knute's Day, January 13.

Poland
In pre-communist Poland, the star of Bethlehem was the most important of the Christmas symbols. The first star to appear on Christmas Eve, it marked the end of the Advent fast and the beginning of the Christmas feast. The village priest, disguised as the "Star Man," would move from home to home asking children to recite their catechism and rewarding them with gifts. He would be accompanied by three boys dressed as the wise men. Following the fall of communism in Poland, old holiday traditions have begun to reappear.

Romania
Romanian children walk from house to house on Christmas Eve giving Christmas greetings and receiving small gifts in return. Families prepare festive dinners, which always include a *turte*, a dessert of paper-thin phyllo dough layered with honey and walnuts. In rural areas, villagers perform reenactments of the story of Herod and the Magi. On Epiphany, January 6, priests make visits to parishioners' homes, dipping sprigs of basil in holy water to sprinkle blessings on the houses and families.

Spain

Christmas in Spain is a raucous time of brightly lighted streets, fancy clothing, and wild celebrations. As darkness falls on Christmas Eve, Spanish families place lamps in their windows as a welcome to Mary and Joseph, the weary travelers. Following midnight worship services, the Spanish begin a celebration of singing, dancing, and dining that lasts most of the night.

Spanish homes include elaborate manger scenes among their decorations. In addition to the standard figures, the Spanish manger scenes include Herod's house, bullfighters, politicians, and usually a stream with a woman kneeling to do laundry. Youngsters receive gifts from the visiting Magi on January 6.

Sweden

Saint Lucia's Day is celebrated throughout Sweden. Centuries ago the story of the young martyr was brought to Sweden, where her remembrance gradually replaced a pagan holiday of the winter solstice. Following the Saint Lucia celebration, preparations begin in earnest for a food-filled Swedish Christmas. Even the birds are included in the feasting, as Swedes place sheaves of wheat in trees or on high poles. The Scandanavian Christmas begins on Saint Lucia's Day, December 13, lasting until Saint Knute's Day, January 13.

United Kingdom

Throughout Great Britain, Christmas could hardly be celebrated without the traditional Christmas goose. Taffy making is also a popular British Christmas custom. In the days when wealthy British families had a large number of servants in their employ, the day after Christmas was reserved as Boxing Day, a day of giving gifts to the hired help. Boxing Day remains a holiday throughout Great Britain.

England. England is the land of wassail, plum puddings, boar's heads, and Christmas caroling. Among other Christmas traditions born in England are the Christmas greeting card, begun in the 1840s, and the custom of hanging Christmas stockings. English children hang their stockings above their beds or at the fireplace on Christmas Eve so that Father Christmas can fill them with treats during the night.

Scotland. Scottish Christmas celebrations are somewhat less elaborate than in England. Scots reserve the greatest merrymaking for New Year's Eve and New Year's Day, a time of family reunions and lengthy celebrations. Traditional menus for the New Year's celebrations include shortbread, black buns, and heavily spiced fruitcake.

Wales. Carol singing is the central theme of a Welsh Christmas. Carols are sung in church, at homes, at the front door of a friend's house, and eventually at a gathering in the town square. Many towns have a contest to see who can create the best new carol. The winner is announced on Christmas Eve as all gather in the town square and sing the new carol along with a host of familiar ones.

LATIN AMERICA

Christmas in Latin America, a land of tremendous cultural diversity, has a flavor all its own. In addition to the culture and language of Spain, Latin America also includes an enormous native population and large communities of European immigrants. As a result, the Christmas holiday has become a mix of religious celebration and pagan festivals. In South American countries, where summer begins in December and winter arrives in June, Christmas is a summer holiday. Parties and celebrations are often outdoor affairs, lasting well into the balmy nights.

Chile

Chileans include a festival of the Virgin Mary with the Christmas customs they share with their South American neighbors. Many years ago, in the town of Andacollo, a woodcutter had a vision in which he was instructed to go to the mountains and await wealth and happiness. He followed the command and, while waiting, carved a three-foot statue of the Virgin. It was placed on an altar where the faithful could come and pray before it. During the Christmas holiday, thousands of visitors come to revere the Virgin, joining the locals in feasting, singing, and dancing.

Colombia

In Colombia, one can count on finding a *pesebre*, or Nativity scene, in nearly all Christian homes. With a background of blue muslin, complete with sewn-in stars, the manger scene may be small and plain or a huge, intricate display, depending on the means of the family. On Christmas Eve, at roughly nine o'clock, Colombians begin to venture from their homes dressed in elaborate costumes for a game of guessing identities. The game ends before midnight, when church bells ring to call worshipers to Christmas Eve services, followed by all-night family feasts. At bedtime, children place their shoes on windowsills, so that the Christ-child and the Magi will leave them gifts.

Mexico

For Mexican families, Christmas festivities begin on December 16, the beginning of the *posadas* holiday. Meaning resting place, or inn, *posadas* is the commemoration of the journey of Mary and Joseph and their search for lodgings in Bethlehem. Homes are richly decorated, and families can expect nightly visits from many friends, family, and fellow church members. The evening invariably ends with the breaking of a piñata, a wildly decorated container filled with toys and candies. Children are blindfolded, given a stick, and instructed to hit the piñata. When it finally breaks, goodies shower down upon the waiting children.

Puerto Rico

After religious celebrations on December 24 and 25, Puerto Rican custom emphasizes the visit of the Magi to the baby Jesus with festivities on January 6, 7, and 8. The three days are a national open house, during which callers go from home to home in an extended party. On Bethlehem Day, January 12, children parade through the streets dressed as the wise men, carrying presents for the infant Christ. While the North American influence of Santa Claus is growing, many families still follow the tradition of giving gifts in the name of the Magi on January 6.

Venezuela

Some years ago, Venezuelans tried to give the Santa Claus tradition a more regional flavor by replacing Father Christmas with a native father character. The effort quickly failed, and today the shoes that children place neatly under their beds on Christmas Eve are filled with candy and toys by Santa Claus.

NORTH AMERICA

Christmas in North America is a patchwork of imported traditions mixed with a few home-grown customs. Immigrants brought Christmas traditions from their homelands, establishing local customs as they settled across the continent.

Canada

Christmas in Canada, like much of Canadian culture, is a mixture of U.S. and British customs. Decorated Christmas trees can be found in most homes, and Canada Post delivers countless Christmas greeting cards. The pre-holiday retail rush sends many Canadians over the border to shop U.S. stores and outlet malls. Yet the Christmas holiday itself is a quiet time of religious observance and family gatherings. Like their British cousins, Canadians observe Boxing Day as an extension of family celebrations.

The United States

Christmas in the United States is a blend of the many traditions imported by immigrants. Americans carry on the German Christmas tree custom, the British Christmas card tradition, and the Danish Christmas Seal practice. Americans have also made the Christmas holiday a national retail event, shopping for gifts, clothing, and seasonal decorations. During the weeks prior to December 25, both local and national media frequently release figures on holiday spending.

Yet despite the materialistic onslaught, many noncommercial Christmas traditions survive. Families flock to performances of Tchaikovsky's *Nutcracker* ballet, Dickens's *A Christmas Carol*, and concerts of Christmas music. The Christmas holiday generally ends with celebrations of New Year's Eve and New Year's Day, though some continue the seasonal observance until Epiphany.

Austria

AS LATELY WE WATCHED

(Die Hirten auf dem Felde)

Traditional Austrian Text

19th Century Austrian Carol

1. As late - ly we watched o'er our field through the night, A
2. A King of such beau - ty was ne'er be - fore seen; And
3. Then shep - herds be joy - ful, sa - lute your dear King; Let
star there was seen, a most glo - ri - ous sight!
Ma - ry, sweet vir - gin, so like to a queen.
hills and dales ring to the song that ye sing:
All through the night, an - gels did sing, In
Blest be the hour, wel - come the morn, For
Blest be the hour, wel - come the morn, For
ca - rols so sweet of the birth of our King.
Christ, our dear Sav - ior, on earth now is born.
Christ, our dear Sav - ior, on earth now is born.

Austria

GLORIA

Traditional Austrian Carol

"Glo - ri - a, Glo - ri - a, To God on high!"
How sweet - ly an - gel hymns Ring through the snow - y sky:
"Glo - ri - a, Glo - ri - a, To God on high!"

Austria

SILENT NIGHT, HOLY NIGHT

(Stille Nacht, heilige Nacht)

Joseph Mohr, 1818
translated by John F. Young

Franz Gruber, 1818

1. Si - lent night, ho - ly night, all is calm, all is bright
2. Si - lent night, ho - ly night, shep - herds quake at the sight;
3. Si - lent night, ho - ly night, Son of God, love's pure light;

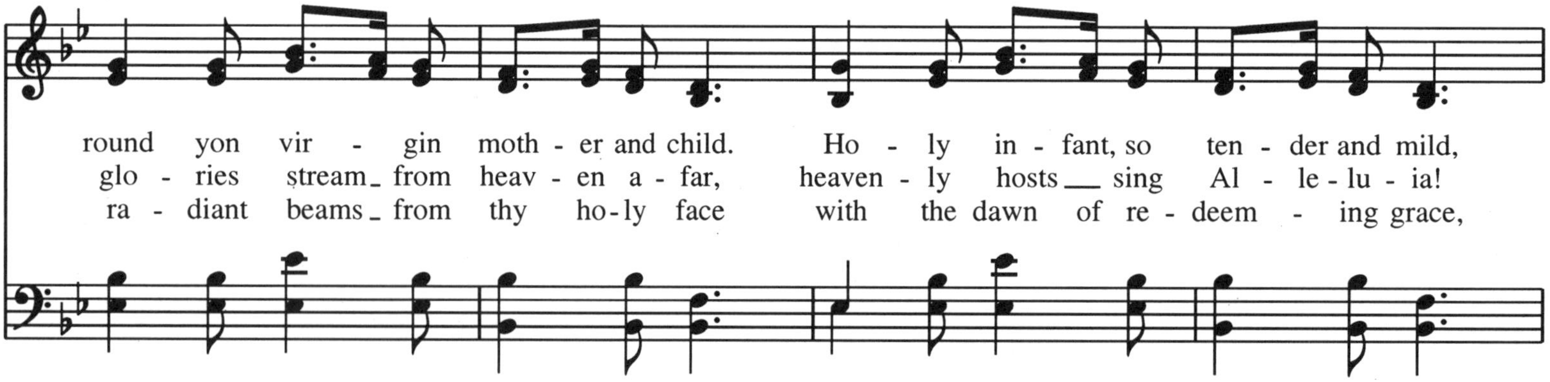
round yon vir - gin moth - er and child. Ho - ly in - fant, so ten - der and mild,
glo - ries stream from heav - en a - far, heaven - ly hosts sing Al - le - lu - ia!
ra - diant beams from thy ho - ly face with the dawn of re - deem - ing grace,

sleep in heav - en - ly peace, sleep in heav - en - ly peace.
Christ the Sav - ior is born, Christ the Sav - ior is born!
Je - sus, Lord, at thy birth, Je - sus, Lord, at thy birth.

Austria

STILL, STILL, STILL

(Still, Still, Still)

Traditional Austrian Text

Melody from Salzburg, c. 1819

1. Still, still, still, He sleeps in this night so still! His
2. Sleep, sleep, sleep, He lies in a slum - ber deep. While
moth - er's car - ing arms en - fold - ing, Warm and safe the ba - by is hold - ing,
an - gel hosts from heav'n come wing - ing, Sweet - est songs of praise they are sing - ing,
Still, still, still, He sleeps in this night so still.
Sleep, sleep, sleep, He lies in a slum - ber deep.

Belgium

THE SIMPLE BIRTH

(De nederige geboorte)

Traditional Flemish Carol

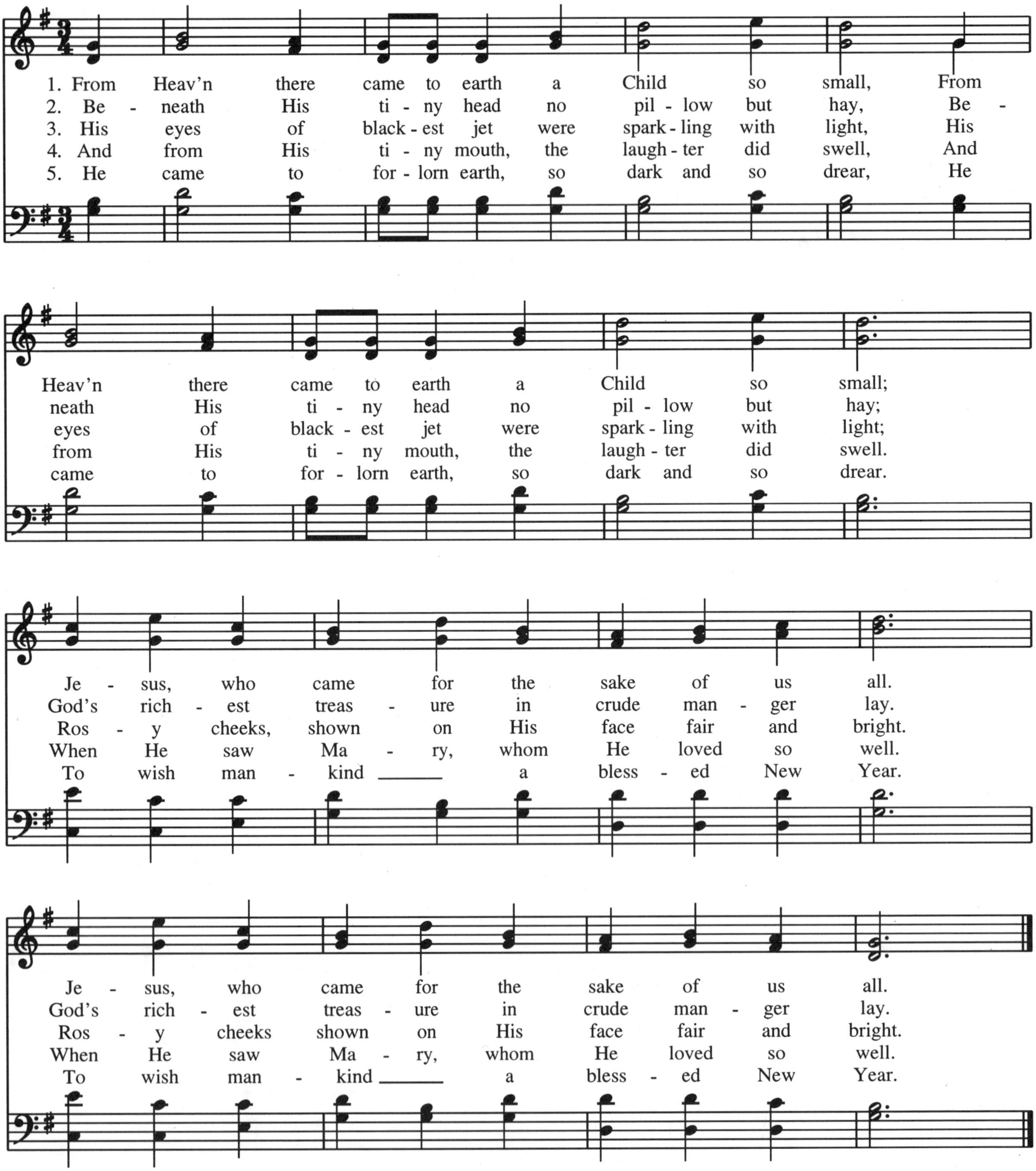
1. From Heav'n there came to earth a Child so small, From
2. Be - neath His ti - ny head no pil - low but hay, Be -
3. His eyes of black - est jet were spark - ling with light, His
4. And from His ti - ny mouth, the laugh - ter did swell, And
5. He came to for - lorn earth, so dark and so drear, He
Heav'n there came to earth a Child so small;
neath His ti - ny head no pil - low but hay;
eyes of black - est jet were spark - ling with light;
from His ti - ny mouth, the laugh - ter did swell.
came to for - lorn earth, so dark and so drear.
Je - sus, who came for the sake of us all.
God's rich - est treas - ure in crude man - ger lay.
Ros - y cheeks, shown on His face fair and bright.
When He saw Ma - ry, whom He loved so well.
To wish man - kind _____ a bless - ed New Year.
Je - sus, who came for the sake of us all.
God's rich - est treas - ure in crude man - ger lay.
Ros - y cheeks, shown on His face fair and bright.
When He saw Ma - ry, whom He loved so well.
To wish man - kind _____ a bless - ed New Year.

Canada

THE HURON CAROL

Traditional French-Canadian Text

Canadian Indian Melody

1. 'Twas in the moon of win - ter - time when all the birds had fled, That
2. With - in a lodge of bro - ken bark the ten - der Babe was found. A
3. The ear - liest moon of win - ter - time is not so round and fair. As
4. O chil - dren of the for - est free, O sons of Man - i - tou, The
might - y Git - chi Man - i - tou sent an - gel choirs in - stead. Be -
rag - ged robe of rab - bit skin en-wrapped His beau - ty 'round; And
was the ring of glo - ry or the help - less In - fant there. The
Ho - ly Child of earth and heav'n is born to - day for you. Come
fore the light the stars grew dim, and won - d'ring hun - ters heard the hymn:
as the hun - ter braves drew nigh, the an - gel song rang loud and high:
chiefs from far be - fore Him knelt with gifts of fur and bea - ver pelt.
kneel be - fore the ra - diant Boy who brings you beau - ty, peace, and joy.
"Je - sus, your King, is born. Je - sus is born. In ex - cel - sis glo - ri - a!"

Canada

WHENCE ART THOU, MY MAIDEN?

(D'où viens-tu, bergère?)

Translation by William McLennan, 1866

Traditional French Canadian

1. "Whence art thou, my maid - en, whence art thou?"
2. "What saw'st thou, my maid - en, what saw'st thou?
3. "Noth - ing more, my maid - en, noth - ing more?
4. "Noth - ing more, my maid - en, noth - ing more?
5. "Noth - ing more, my maid - en, noth - ing more?
"I come from the sta - ble where, this ver - y night,
"There with - in a man - ger, a ti - ny Child I saw,
"There I saw the vir - gin, her sweet Ba - by hold,
"I saw ass and ox - en, kneel - ing meek and mild,
"There were three bright an - gels, come down from the sky,
I, a shep - herd maid - en, saw a marv' - lous sight."
Ly - ing soft - ly sleep - ing, on a bed of straw."
And the fa - ther, Jo - seph, trem - bling with the cold."
Soft - ly their breath - ing, warmed the ho - ly Child."
Sing - ing forth great prais - es, to our God on high."

Colombia

QUICKLY NOW, O SHEPHERDS

(Vamos, pastorcitos)

Traditional Colombian Carol

1. Quick - ly now, O shep - herds, Go to Beth - le - hem!
2. Such a lit - tle Ba - by, Born this ho - ly day!
3. Has - ten now, O shep - herds, Has - ten to a - dore!

There to see the Vir - gin, And her ho - ly Son.
Cheer Him with your sing - ing, Of a lull - a - by.
Je - sus, gift of Heav - en, Lord for - ev - er - more!

Chile

GOING TO BETHLEHEM

(Vamos a Belén)

Traditional Chilean Carol

1. Good eve - ning, dear, gen-tle Ma - ry, My heart is filled with de -
2. Good - bye to you lit-tle Man - uel, Un - til the New Year be -
3. O Ma - ry, Ho - li-est Mo - ther, As pure as flow - ers un -
vo - tion, My heart is filled with de - vo - tion; For
gin - ning, Un - til the New Year be - gin - ning; I'll
fold - ing, As pure as flow - ers un - fold - ing; I
you and Je - sus so love - ly, A fer - vent prayer I am
see you af - ter the shear - ing, So rich from wool you'll be
come on this eve of Christ - mas, Thy love and glo - ry be -
off - 'ring, A fer - vent prayer I am off - 'ring.
sell - ing, So rich from wool you'll be sell - ing.
hold - ing, Thy love and glo - ry be - hold - ing.

Refrain
Go - ing, go - ing, to Beth - le - hem town, Go - ing, go - ing the ba - by to
see, To greet his fa - ther, Jo - seph, and
1, 2
Ma - ry, on bend - ed knee.
3
Ma - ry, on bend - ed knee.

Croatia

HEAR, O SHEPHERDS

Traditional Croation Carol

Hear, O shep - herds, hear while I tell you, Hark to the mir - a - cle that
on - ly now be - fell you: On a man - ger low - ly, In a prick - ly stall
Lies the ba - by ho - ly Who will save us all.
Lies the ba - by ho - ly Who will save us all.

Czech Republic

COME, ALL YE SHEPHERDS

(Nesem Vam Noviny)

Traditional Czech Text

Moravian Melody

1. Come, all ye shep - herds, your flocks will not stray,
2. Has - ten to Beth - le - hem, there to be - hold
Come and see Je - sus a - sleep on the hay
The Christ - child whose com - ing an - gels fore - told.
Near the dark man - ger sits His moth - er mild, Hum - ming she hov - ers
"Peace on the earth and good will to all men," That is the mes - sage
o'er her pre - cious Child; Come, with - out fear!
sent down from heav - en; O praise the Lord!

Czech Republic

FROM OUT THE DEEP WOODS A CUCKOO FLEW

(Zezulka z Lesa Vyl′tla)

Traditional Czech Carol

1. From out the deep woods a cuck - oo flew, Cuck - oo!
2. High in the raft - ers there sat a dove, Coo - roo!
Seek - ing the heav - en - ly Babe to woo, Cuck - oo! Near
Coo - ing to Je - sus of his great love, Coo - roo! His
Je - sus' bed, he gave in songs The praise that
heart and voice so full of joy That Heav - en
to our God be - longs, Cuck - oo, cuck - oo, cuck - oo!
sent this love - ly Boy! Coo - roo, coo - roo, coo - roo!

Czech Republic

I GO TO BETHLEHEM

(Sel Bych Rád k Betlému)

Traditional Czech Carol

I go to Beth - le - hem, To see the ti - ny child;
Roos - ter will crow a - way Mak - ing the Ba - by gay;
My black roos - ter, trim and sleek, My cuck - oo with
Cuck - oo perch - ing near His lit - tle head, Call - ing, soft - ly will
song so sweet: These will I give Him.
make His heart glad: These will I give Him.
Coo, coo-coo! (p - echo) Coo, coo-coo! Je - sus, He sings for you!
Coo, coo-coo! (p - echo) Coo coo-coo Je - sus, He sings for you!

Czech Republic

LET OUR GLADNESS KNOW NO END

Traditional Bohemian Carol

1. Let our glad - ness know no end, Hal - le - lu - jah!
2. See the love - l'est bloom - ing rose, Hal - le - lu - jah!
3. In - to flesh is made the word, Hal - le - lu - jah!
Un - to earth did Christ de - scend, Hal - le - lu - jah.
From the branch of Jes - se grows, Hal - le - lu - jah.
'Tis our re - fuge, Christ the Lord, Hal - le - lu - jah.
On this day God gave us. Christ His Son to save us.
Christ, His
Christ, His Son, His Son to save us.

Czech Republic

ROCKING

(Hajej, Hyneh, Jezisku)

Traditional Czech Carol

1. Ba - by Je - sus, gent - ly sleep, do not stir;
2. Ma - ry's pre - cious ba - by sleep, gent - ly sleep,
We will bring a coat of fur.
Sleep in com - fort, slum - ber deep.
We will rock you,
rock you, rock you, Gent - ly slum - ber as we rock you,
See the fur to keep you warm, Snug - ly fits your ti - ny form.
We will praise you all we can, Dar - ling, dar - ling lit - tle man.

Denmark

A CHILD IS BORN IN BETHLEHEM

(Et Barn er Født i Bethlehem)

Nicolai F.S. Grundtvig, 1783-1872

Traditional Danish Carol
adapted from 14th-Century Latin Text

1. A child is born in Beth - le - hem, in Beth - le - hem; And peace is in Je - ru - sa - lem,
2. A low - ly maid - en with - out home, with - out a home; Gave birth to God's own Ho - ly Son,
3. She chose a man - ger for his bed, for Je - sus' bed; God's an - gels sang of joy o'er - head,
4. Give thanks and praise e - ter - nal - ly, e - ter - nal - y; To God the Ho - ly Trin - i - ty,
Al - le - lu - ia, al - le - lu - ia!

Denmark

CHILD JESUS

(Barn Jesus)

Hans Christian Andersen, 1805-1875

Niels Gade, 1817-1890

1. Child Je - sus in a man - ger lay, Yet Heav - en was His
2. O crip - pled soul be glad to - day, Cast out your bit - ter
own; His low - ly pil - low was of straw, And
pain; For Beth - le'm's Babe will show the way, We
'round Him no light shone. But Heav - en sent a
heav'n - ly bliss can gain. Let us with child - like
star so bright, And ox - en kissed his feet that night,
heart and mind, Seek now the Son of God to find.
Al - le - lu - ia, Al - le - lu - ia, Al - le - lu - ia!

Denmark

LOVELY IS THE DARK BLUE SKY

(Deilig Er den Himmel Blaa)

Nicolai F.S. Grundtvig

Traditional Danish Carol

1. Love - ly is the dark blue sky, Ma - gi - cal to
2. On the ear - liest Christ - mas night, All the stars were
3. Wise men from the East a - far, Led to Je - sus
ev - 'ry eye, Where the gold - en stars are blink - ing,
shin - ing bright, When a - mong them, burst in bril - liance,
by the star, There a - dor - ing Heav'n's e - lec - ted,
See them smil - ing, see them wink - ing. Beck - 'ning us to
One lone star whose stream - ing ra - diance Far out - shown the
Found with - in his soul di - rect - ed. God's great Light, and
Heav'n on high, Beck - 'ning us to Heav'n on high.
sun's own light, Far out - shown the sun's own light.
Love, and Pow'r. God's great Light, and Love, and Pow'r.

England

AS WITH GLADNESS MEN OF OLD

William Chatterton Dix

melody by Conrad Kocher
harmonized for The English Hymnal, 1906

1. As with gladness men of old did the
2. As with joyful steps they sped to that
3. As they offered gifts most rare at that
4. Holy Jesus! every day keep us
5. In the heavenly country bright, need they
guiding star behold; as with joy they hailed its
lowly manger bed; there to bend the knee be-
manger rude and bare; so may we with holy
in the narrow way; and, when earthly things are
no created light; thou its light, its joy, its
light, leading onward, beaming bright; so, most
fore him whom heaven and earth adore; so may
joy, pure and free from sin's alloy, all our
past, bring our ransomed souls at last where they
crown, thou its sun which goes not down: there for-
gracious Lord, may we evermore be led to thee.
we with willing feet ever seek the mercy-seat.
costliest treasures bring, Christ! to thee, our heavenly King.
need no star to guide, where no clouds thy glory hide.
ever may we sing alleluias to our King.

England

AWAY IN A MANGER

author unknown

melody by William James Kirkpatrick
(1838-1921)

(unison)
1. A - way in a manger, no crib for his bed, the
2. The cat - tle are low - ing, the ba - by a - wakes, but
3. Be near me, Lord Je - sus; I ask thee to stay close
lit - tle Lord Je - sus laid down his sweet head. The
lit - tle Lord Je - sus no cry - ing he makes. I
by me for - ev - er, and love me I pray. Bless
stars in the bright sky looked down where he lay, the
love thee, Lord Je - sus! Look down from the sky, and
all the dear chil - dren in thy ten - der care, and
lit - tle Lord Je - sus a - sleep on the hay.
stay by my side un - til morn - ing is nigh.
fit us for heav - en to live with thee there.

England

THE BOAR'S HEAD CAROL

19th Century English Carol

1. The boar's head in hand bear I, Be - decked with bays and rose - ma - ry; And I
2. The boar's head as I un - der - stand is the fin - est dish in all the land, When
3. Our stew - ard hath pro - vid - ed this In hon - or of the King of Bliss, Which
pray you, my mas - ters, be mer - ry, *Quot es - tis in con - vi - vi - o,
thus be - decked with a gay gar - land, Let us ser - vi - re can - ti - co.
on this day to be serv - ed is, In Re - gi - nen - si a - tri - o.
Ca - put a - pri de - fe - ro, Red - dens lau - des Do - mi - no.

*translations: Verse 1 - You who are at this feast;
Verse 2 - Serve by singing;
Verse 3 - In the royal hall.

Versions of this carol date as far back as the 15th century.
This edition presents the version used at Queen's College, Oxford, published in 1812.

England

THE CHERRY TREE CAROL

Tradtional English Carol

1. As Jo - seph was a - walk - ing He heard an - gels
2. "His birth - bed shall be nei - ther In house nor in
3. "He nei - ther shall be cloth - ed In pur - ple nor
4. "He nei - ther shall be christ - en'd In milk nor in
sing; "This shall be the birth - night Of Christ, our heav'n-ly King.
hall, Nei - ther in Par - a - dise, But in an ox - en's stall.
pall; But all in fair lin - en, As wear young ba - bies all.
wine, But in pure sweet wa - ter, Fresh spring - ing from Be - thine."

*There are at least four tunes to these words.
The carol can contain as many as 18 verses.

England

COVENTRY CAROL

Robert Croo, 1543

English Melody, 1591

1., 5. Lul - lay, Thou lit - tle ti - ny Child,
2. O sis - ters, too, how may we do,
3. Her - od the King, in his rag - ing,
4. Then woe is me, poor Child, for Thee,
By, by, lul - ly, lul - lay; Lul -
For to pre - serve this day; This
Charg - ed he hath this day; His
And ev - er mourn and say; For
lay, Thou lit - tle ti - ny Child,
poor Young - ling for whom we sing,
men of might, in his own sight,
Thy part - ing nor say nor sing,
By, by, lul - ly, lul - lay.
By, by, lul - ly, lul - lay.
All chil - dren young, to slay.
By, by, lul - ly, lul - lay.

England

THE FIRST NOWELL

17th Century English Carol
arranged by John Stainer, 1871

1. The first No - well the angel did say was to
2. They look - ed up and saw a star shin-ing
3. And by the light of that same star three
4. This star drew nigh to the north - west, o'er
5. Then en - tered in those wise men three full
6. Then let us all with one ac - cord sing
cer - tain poor shep - herds in fields as they lay; in
in the east be - yond them far, and
wise men came from coun - try far; to
Beth - le - hem it took its rest, and
rev - erent - ly up - on their knee, and
prais - es to our heav - en - ly Lord; that
fields as they lay, keep - ing their sheep, on a
to the earth it gave great light, and
seek for a king was their in - tent, and to
there it did both stop and stay right
of - fered there in his pres - ence their
hath made heaven and earth of nought and

cold win - ter's night that was so deep.
so it con - tin - ued both day and night.
fol - low the star wher - ev - er it went.
o - ver the place where Je - sus lay.
gold, and myrrh, and frank - in - cense.
with his blood man - kind hath bought.
No -
well, No - well, No - well, No - well,
born is the King of Is - ra - el.

England

GOD REST YOU MERRY, GENTLEMEN

19th Century English Carol

1. God rest you mer - ry, gen - tle - men, Let noth - ing you dis -
2. In Beth - le - hem, in Jew - ry, This bless - ed Babe was
3. From God, our heav'n - ly Fa - ther, A bless - ed an - gel
4. The shep - herds at those ti - dings, Re - joic - ed much in
may, Re - mem - ber, Christ, our Sav - ior, Was born on Christ - mas
born, And laid with - in a man - ger Up - on this bless - ed
came, And un - to cer - tain shep - herds Brought ti - dings of the
mind, And left their flocks a - feed - ing, In tem - pest, storm, and
day; To save us all from Sa - tan's pow'r, When we were gone a -
morn; The which His moth - er Ma - ry Did noth - ing take in
same; How that in Beth - le - hem was born The Son of God by
wind, And went to Beth - le - hem strait - way, The Son of God to
stray.
scorn.
name.
find.
O ti - dings of com - fort and joy, com-fort and

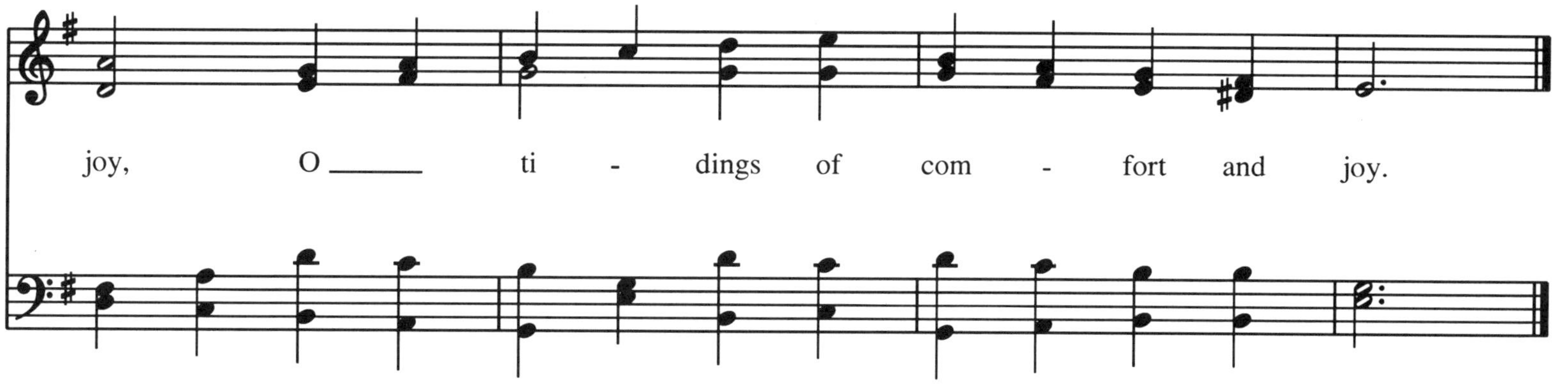
joy, O ___ ti - dings of com - fort and joy.

5. Now when they came to Bethlehem, Where our sweet Saviour lay,
They found him in a manger, Where oxen feed on hay,
The blessed Virgin kneeling down, Unto the Lord did pray.
And it's tidings of comfort and joy.

6. With sudden joy and gladness, The shepherds were beguil'd,
To see the Babe of Israel, Before his mother mild,
On them with joy and cheerfulness, Rejoice each mother's child.
And it's tidings of comfort and joy.

7. Now to the Lord sing praises, All you within this place,
Like we true loving brethren, Each other to embrace,
For the merry time of Christmas, Is drawing on a pace.
And it's tidings of comfort and joy.

8. God bless the ruler of this house, And send him long to reign,
And many a merry Christmas may live to see again.
Among your friends and kindred, That live both far and near,
And God send you a happy New Year.

England

THE GOLDEN CAROL

Old English Carol

1. We saw a light shine out a - far, On Christ - mas in the
2. Oh! ev - er thought be of His Name, On Christ - mas in the
morn - ing, And straight we knew it was Christ's star, Bright
morn - ing, Who bore for us both grief and shame, Af -
beam - ing in the morn - ing. Then did we fall on
flic - tions sharp - est scorn - ing. And may we die (when
bend - ed knee, On Christ - mas in the morn - ing, And
death shall come), On Christ - mas in the morn - ing, And
prais'd the Lord, who'd let us see His glo - ry at its dawn - ing.
see in heav'n, our glo - ri'us home, That Star of Christ - mas morn - ing.

England

GOOD KING WENCESLAS

John M. Neale, 1853

Piae Cantiones, 1582
(originally a spring carol)

1. Good King Wen - ces - las look'd out On the Feast of Ste - phen,
2. "Hith - er, page, and stand by me, If thou know'st it; tell - ing,
3. "Bring me flesh, and bring me wine, Bring me pine - logs hith - er;
4. "Sire, the night is dark - er now, And the wind blows strong - er;
5. In his mas - ter's steps he trod, Where the snow lay dint - ed;
When the snow lay round a - bout, Deep and crisp, and e - ven:
Yon - der peas - ant, who is he? Where and what his dwell - ing?"
Thou and I will see him dine, When we bear them thith - er."
Fails my heart, I know not how, I can go no long - er."
Heat was in the ver - y sod Which the saint had print - ed.
Bright - ly shone the moon that night, Though the frost was cru - el,
"Sire, he lives a good league hence, Un - der - neath the moun - tain;
Page and mon - arch forth they went, Forth they went to - geth - er;
"Mark my foot - steps, my good page, Tread thou in them bold - ly:
There - fore, Chris - tian men, be sure, Wealth or rank pos - sess - ing,
When a poor man came in sight, Gath - 'ring win - ter fu - el.
Right a - gainst the for - est fence, By Saint Ag - nes' foun - tain."
Through the rude wind's wild la - ment, And the bit - ter weath - er.
Thou shalt find the win - ter's rage, Freeze thy blood less cold - ly."
Ye who now will bless the poor, Shall your - selves find bless - ing.

England

THE HOLLY AND THE IVY

18th Century English Carol

1. The hol - ly and the i - vy, When they are both full grown, Of
2. The hol - ly bears a blos - som, As white as li - ly flow'r, And
3. The hol - ly bears a ber - ry, As red as an - y blood, And
4. The hol - ly bears a prick - le, As sharp as an - y thorn, And
5. The hol - ly bears a bark, As bit - ter as the gall, And
6. The hol - ly and the i - vy, When they are both full grown, Of
all the trees that are in the wood, The hol - ly bears the crown:
Ma - ry bore sweet Je - sus Christ, To be our dear Sav - ior:
Ma - ry bore sweet Je - sus Christ, To do poor sin - ners good:
Ma - ry bore sweet Je - sus Christ, On Christ-mas day in the morn:
Ma - ry bore sweet Je - sus Christ, For to re - deem us all:
all the trees that are in the wood, The hol - ly bears the crown:
The ris - ing of the sun and the run-ning of the deer, The
play - ing of the mer - ry or - gan, Sweet sing - ing in the choir.

England

I SAW THREE SHIPS

Traditional English Carol
arranged by John Stainer, 1871

1. I saw three ships come sail - ing in,
2. And what was in those ships all three?
3. Our Sav - ior Christ and His la - dy.
4. Pray, whith - er sailed those ships all three?
On Christ - mas Day, on Christ - mas Day;
I saw three ships come sail - ing in,
And what was in those ships all three?
Our Sav - ior Christ and His la - dy,
Pray, whith - er sailed those ships all three?
On Christ - mas Day in the morn - ing.

5. O, they sailed in to Bethlehem,
On Christmas Day, on Christmas Day,
O, they sailed in to Bethlehem,
On Christmas Day in the morning.

6. And all the bells on earth shall ring,
On Christmas Day, on Christmas Day,
And all the bells on earth shall ring,
On Christmas Day in the morning.

7. And all the angels in Heav'n shall sing,
On Christmas Day, on Christmas Day,
And all the angels in Heav'n shall sing,
On Christmas Day in the morning.

8. And all the souls on earth shall sing,
On Christmas Day, on Christmas Day,
And all the souls on earth shall sing,
On Christmas Day in the morning.

9. Then let us all rejoice amain!
On Christmas Day, on Christmas Day,
Then let us all rejoice amain!
On Christmas Day in the morning.

England

IN THE BLEAK MIDWINTER

Poem by Christina Rossetti, 1872

Gustav Holst, 1906

1. In the bleak mid - win - ter, frost - y wind made moan,
2. Our God, heaven can - not hold him, nor ___ earth sus - tain;
3. An - gels and arch - an - gels may have gath - ered there,
4. What ___ can I give him, poor ___ as I am?
earth stood hard as i - ron, wa - ter like a stone;
heaven and earth shall flee a - way when he comes to reign.
cher - u - bim and ser - a - phim throng - ed the air;
If I were a shep - herd, I would bring a lamb;
snow had fall - en, snow on snow, snow ___ on ___ snow,
In the bleak mid - win - ter a sta - ble place suf - ficed the
but his moth - er on - ly, in her maid - en bliss,
if I were a Wise Man, I would do my part; yet
in the bleak mid - win - ter, long ___ a - go.
Lord ___ God Al - might - y, Je - sus Christ.
wor - shiped the be - lov - ed with ___ a kiss.
what I can I give him: give ___ my heart.

England

IT CAME UPON THE MIDNIGHT CLEAR

Edmund H. Sears (1810-1876)

English Melody
adapted by Arthur Sullivan

1. It came up - on the mid - night clear, that glo - rious song of old, from
2. Still through the clov - en skies they come with peace - ful wings un - furled, and
3. Yet with the woes of sin and strife the world has suf - fered long; be -
4. For lo! the days are haste - ning on, by pro - phets seen of old, when
an - gels bend ing - near the earth to touch their harps of gold: "Peace
still their heaven - ly mu - sic floats o'er all the wea - ry world; a -
neath the heaven - ly hymn have rolled two - thou - sand years of wrong; and
with the ev - er - cir - cling years shall come the time fore - told, when
on the earth, good will to men, from heaven's all - gra - cious King." The
bove its sad and low - ly plains they bend on hov - ering wing, and
war - ring hu - man - kind hears not the tid - ings which they bring; O
peace shall o - ver all the earth its an - cient splen - dors fling, and
world in sol - emn still - ness lay to hear the an - gels sing.
ev - er o'er its Ba - bel sounds the bless - ed an - gels sing.
hush the noise and cease . your strife and hear the an - gels sing!
all the world give back the song which now the an - gels sing.

England

ONCE IN ROYAL DAVID'S CITY

Cecil Frances Alexander, 1848

Henry J. Gauntlett, 1849

1. Once in roy - al Da - vid's cit - y stood a low - ly cat - tle
2. He came down to earth from heav - en who is God and Lord of
3. Je - sus is our child - hood's pat - tern; day by day, like us he
4. And our eyes at last shall see him, through his own re-deem - ing
shed, where a moth - er laid her ba - by in a
all, and his shel - ter was a sta - ble, and his
grew; he was lit - tle, weak, and help - less, tears and
love; for that child so dear and gen - tle is our
man - ger for his bed; Ma - ry, lov - ing moth - er
cra - dle was a stall. With the poor, the scorned, the
smiles like us he knew; and he feel - eth for our
Lord in heav - en a - bove; and he leads his chil - dren
mild, Je - sus Christ, her lit - tle child.
low - ly lived on earth our Sav - ior ho - ly.
sad - ness, and he shar - eth in our glad - ness.
on to the place where he is gone.

England

SUSSEX CAROL

Traditional English Carol
arranged by Ralph Vaughn Williams, 1919

(unison)
1. On Christ - mas night all Chris - tians sing, To
2. Then why should men on earth be so sad, Since
3. When sin de - parts be - fore ___ his grace, Then
4. All out of dark - ness we ___ have light, Which
hear the news ___ the an - gels bring; On Christ - mas night all
our Re - deem - er made us glad, Then why should men on
life and health ___ come in its place; When sin de - parts be -
made the an - gels sing this night; All out of dark - ness
Chris - tians sing, To hear the news ___ the an - gels bring
earth be so sad, Since our Re - deem - er made us glad,
fore ___ his grace, Then life and health ___ come in its place;
we ___ have light, Which made the an - gels sing this night;
News of great joy, ___ news of ___ great mirth,
When from our sin ___ he set ___ us free,
An - gels and men ___ with joy ___ may sing,
"Glo - ry to God ___ and peace ___ to men,
News of our mer - ci - ful ___ King's birth. ___
All for to gain our li - ber - ty. ___
All for to see the new - born King. ___
Now and for - ev - er _ more. ___ A - men." ___

England

WASSAIL SONG

Traditional English Carol
arranged by John Stainer, 1871

1. Here we come a - was - sail - ing A - mong the leaves so green; Here we come a - wan - d'ring, So fair to be seen.
2. We are not dai - ly beg - gars That beg from door to door; But we are neigh - bor's chil - dren, Whom you have seen be - fore.
3. Good mas - ter and mis - tress, As you sit by the fire, Pray think of us poor chil - dren, Who wan - der in the mire.
4. God bless the mas - ter of this house, Like - wise the mis - tress, too, And all the lit - tle chil - dren, That round the ta - ble go.
Love and joy come to you, And to you glad Christ - mas too; And God bless you and send you a hap - py New Year, And God send you a hap - py New Year.

England

WASSAIL, WASSAIL

Old English Air

1. Was - sail, Was - sail all o - ver the town! Our bread it is white and our ale it is brown; Our bowl is made of the ma - ple tree, So here my good fel - low, I'll drink to thee.
2. The was - s'ling bowl with a toast with - in, Come, fill it up now un - to the brim. Come, fill it up that we may all see, With the was - sail - ing bowl, I'll drink to thee.
3. Come but - ler bring us a bowl of your best, And we hope your soul in heav - en shall rest. But if you bring us a bowl too small, Then down shall go but - ler and bowl and all.

England

WE WISH YOU A MERRY CHRISTMAS

English Folksong

We wish you a Mer-ry Christ-mas, We wish you a Mer-ry Christ-mas, We
Fine
wish you a Mer-ry Christ-mas, And a hap-py New Year! Good ti-dings to
D.C. al Fine
you wher-ev-er you are; Good ti-dings for Christ-mas and a hap-py New Year!

England

WHAT CHILD IS THIS?

William C. Dix, 1865

Greensleeves, 16th Century English Melody

1. What child is this who, laid to rest, on
2. Why lies he in such mean es - tate where
3. So bring him in - cense, gold, and myrrh, come,
Ma - ry's lap is sleep - ing? Whom an - gels greet with
ox and ass are feed - ing? Good Chris - tians, fear, for
peas - ant, king, to own him; the King of kings sal -
an - thems sweet, while shep - herds watch are keep - ing?
sin - ners here the si - lent Word is plead - ing.
va - tion brings, let lov - ing hearts en - throne him.
This, this is Christ the King, whom shep - herds guard and an - gels sing;
haste, haste to bring him laud, the babe, the son of Ma - ry.

France

ANGELS WE HAVE HEARD ON HIGH

(Les anges dans nos campagnes)

19th Century French Carol

1. An - gels we have heard on high Sweet - ly sing - ing o'er the plains,
2. Shep - herds, why this ju - bi - lee? Why your joy - ous strains pro - long?
3. Come to Beth - le - hem and see Him whose birth the an - gels sing;
And the moun - tains in re - ply Ech - o - ing their joy - ous strains.
What the glad - some ti - dings be Which in - spire your heav'n - ly song?
Come, a - dore on bend - ed knee Christ, the Lord, the new - born King.
Glo - - - - - - - - - - ri - a
in ex - cel - sis De - o,
Glo - - - - - - - - - - - - - - ri - a
in ex - cel - sis De - o.

France

BRING A TORCH, JEANNETTE, ISABELLE

(Un flambeau, Jeannette, Isabelle)

translated by E. Cuthbert Nunn (1868-1914)

17th Century Provençal Carol

1. Bring a torch, Jean - nette, Is - a - bel - la, Bring a
2. It is wrong when the Child is sleep - ing, It is
3. Soft - ly to the lit - tle sta - ble, Soft - ly
torch, to the cra - dle run! It is Je - sus, good
wrong to talk so loud. Si - lence all, as you
for the mo - ment come; Look and see how
folk of the vil - lage; Christ is born and Ma - ry's
gath - er a - round them, Lest your noise should wa - ken
charm - ing is Je - sus, How he is pure, his cheeks are
call - ing. Ah! Ah! Beau - ti - ful is the Moth - er.
Je - sus. Hush! Hush! See how fast he slum - bers.
ro - sy. Hush! Hush! See how the child is sleep - ing.
Ah! Ah! Beau - ti - ful is her Son.
Hush! Hush! See how fast he sleeps.
Hush! Hush! See how he smiles in dreams.

France

HE IS BORN, THE DIVINE CHRIST CHILD

(Il est né, le divin enfant)

Traditional 19th-Century French

18th Century French Carol

He is born, the di - vine Christ child. Play on the o - boe and bag - pipes
mer - ri - ly. He is born, the di - vine Christ child. Sing we all of the
Sa - vior's birth.
Fine
1. Through long a - ges of the past,
2. Oh, how love - ly, oh, how pure.
3. Je - sus, Lord of all the world,
Proph - ets have fore - told his com - ing; Through long a - ges
Is this per - fect child of heav - en. Oh, how love - ly,
Com - ing as a child a - mong us, Je - sus, Lord of
D.C. al Fine
of the past, Now the time has come at last.
oh, how pure, Gra - cious gift of God, to man.
all the world, Grant to us Thy heav'n - ly peace.

France

INFANT SO GENTLE

Gascon Carol

1. In - fant so gen - tle, so pure and so sweet
2. In - fant so ho - ly, so meak and so mild,
Love from Thy ti - ny eyes sin - ners doth greet,
We come to wel - come Thee, our dear Christ child.
Ten - d'rest words fail all Thy beau - ty to show
We can - not tell Thee how much we do need,
We must a - dore Thee, if Thee we would know.
Thy pre - cious pre - sence; all sin - ners take heed.

France

MARCH OF THE THREE KINGS

M.L. Hohman, 1937

Provençal, 13th Century

(unison)
(parts)
1. Three great kings _ came from the O - ri - ent, _ A star full bright _ showed _ them the
2. And we saw _ the star stop o'er a stall, _ Its bright light sent _ forth _ a ho -
(unison)
(parts)
high - way; _ Robed were they _ in cost - li - est rai - ment, _ With crowns and
ly _ glow; _ It re - veal'd _ the Babe so dear and small, _ In swad - dling
jew - els in a fine dis - play; And they car - ried gifts in casks of
gar-ments in a man - ger low. We bow'd our knees in won-der - ous
gold _ For the low - born Christ - child _ we were told, _ And we join'd
awe, _ Sing-ing God's prais - es, _ "Al - le - lu - ia," _ For His shin -
their band and march'd with them _ To find the ho - ly child of Beth - le - hem.
ing star led three wise men _ To find the ho - ly child of Beth - le - hem.

France

NOËL NOUVELET

Traditional French Carol

1. Christ - mas comes a - gain, oh sing we ___ all No - el! Glo - ry be to God, now let ___ our prais - es swell!
2. An - gels did pro - claim, oh shep - herds ___ come and see, Born in Beth - le - hem a bles - sed ___ Lamb for thee.
3. In the man - ger bare the shep - herds ___ found the child, Jo - seph stood well there with Mar - y, ___ Moth - er mild.
Sing we No - el for Christ the new - born King, No - el.
Christ - mas comes a - gain, oh sing we ___ all No - el.

France

O COME, O COME, IMMANUEL

12th Century, French

Gregorian, 8th Century

1. O come, O come, Im - man - u - el, And ran - som cap - tive
2. O come, Thou Rod of Jes - se, free Thine own from Sa - tan's
3. O come, Thou Day-Spring, come and cheer Our spir - its by Thine
4. O come, Thou Key of Da - vid, come, And o - pen wide our
5. O come, O come, Thou Lord of might, Who to Thy tribes, on
Is - ra - el, That mourns in lone - ly ex - ile
tyr - an - ny; From depths of hell thy peo - ple
ad - vent here; Dis - perse the gloom - y clouds of
heav'n - ly home; Make safe the way that leads on
Si - nai's height, In an - cient times did'st give the
here Un - til the Son of God ap - pear.
save, And give them vic - t'ry o'er the grave.
night, And death's dark shad - ows put to flight.
high, And close the path to mis - er - y.
Law, In cloud, and maj - es - ty and awe.
Re - joice! Re - joice! Im - man - u - el Shall come to thee, O Is - ra - el.

France

O LEAVE YOUR SHEEP

(Quittez, pasteurs)

Traditional French Carol

1. O leave your sheep, ye shep - herds come a -
2. O see him there, so tin - y and so
way, from your flocks come, your sheep and lambs will
weak, a lit - tle babe with - in a man - ger
stay. O stop your tears, Your souls with joy re -
laid. From heav'n a - bove He comes the earth to
new. Come, hur - ry to a - dore the one, the
save As God's in - car - nate Word. He is, he
one, the one who comes to com - fort you.
is Our Lord and our faith - ful shep - herd.

France

O HOLY NIGHT

(Cantique de Noël)

Placide Cappeau
translated by John S. Dwight

Adolphe Adam, 1847
published posthumously, 1858

1. O ho - ly night! the stars are bright - ly shin - ing. It is the
2. Led by the light of faith se - rene - ly beam - ing, With glow - ing
3. Tru - ly He taught us to love one an - oth - er; His law is
night of the dear Sav - ior's birth; Long lay the world in sin and er - ror
hearts by His cra - dle we stand; So led by light of a star sweet - ly
love and His gos - pel is peace; Chains shall He break, for the slave is our
pin - ing, Till He ap - peared and the soul felt its worth. A
gleam - ing, Here came the wise men from O - ri - ent land. The
broth - er, And in His name all op - pres - sion shall cease. Sweet
thrill of hope the wea - ry world re - joic - es, For yon - der breaks a
King of kings lay thus in low - ly man - ger, In all our tri - als
hymns of joy in grate - ful chor - us raise we, Let all with - in us

new and glo - rious morn; Fall on your knees, Oh, _
born to be our Friend; He knows our need, To our
praise His ho - ly name; Christ is the Lord, Oh, _
hear _ the an - gel voic - es! O night _ di -
weak - ness is no strang - er. Be - hold _ your
praise _ His name for - ev - er! His pow'r _ and
vine, _ O night _ when Christ was born! O
King, _ be - fore _ Him low - ly bend! Be -
glo - ry ev - er - more pro - claim! His
(3rd verse)
night, O ho - ly night, O night, di - vine!
hold your King, be - fore Him low - ly bend!
pow'r and glo - ry ev - er - more pro - claim.

France

PAT-A-PAN

Bernard de la Mannoye
Burgundian, c. 1700

(unison)
1. Wil - lie, take your lit - tle drum, Rob - in bring your whis - tle, come. When we hear the fife and drum. Tu - re - lu - re - lu, pat - a - pat - a - pan. When we hear the fife and drum, Christ-mas should be ___ light and fun.
2. Thus the men of ol - den days gave the King of Kings their praise, When they hear the fife and drum. Tu - re - lu - re - lu, pat - a - pat - a - pan. With the drums they sing and play, Full of joy on ___ Christ - mas Day.
3. God and Man are now be - come close - ly joined as fife and drum, When we play the fife and drum. Tu - re - lu - re - lu, pat - a - pat - a - pan. When on fife and drum we play, Dance and make the ___ hol - i - day,

France

SHEPHERD! SHAKE OFF YOUR DROWSY SLEEP

(Berger, secoue ton sommeil profond)

Traditional French

Traditional Besançon Carol

1. Shep - herd, shake off your drow - sy sleep, Rise and
2. See how the flow'rs all burst a - new, Think - ing
3. Shep - herd, then up and quick a - way! Seek the
leave your sil - ly sheep; An - gels from Heav'n a - round are
snow is sum - mer dew; See how the stars a - fresh are
Babe ere break of day. He is the hope of ev - 'ry
sing - ing, Tid - ings of great joy are bring - ing.
glow - ing, All their bright - est beams be - stow - ing.
na - tion, All in Him shall find sal - va - tion.
Refrain
Shep-herd! The cho - rus come and swell! Sing No - el, O sing No - el!

France

THE SLEEP OF THE INFANT JESUS

(Le sommeil de l'enfant Jésus)

Traditional French Carol

1. Here, 'mid the ass and ox - en mild,
2. Here, 'mid the rose and lil - y bright,
3. Here, 'mid the shep - herds' glad de - light,
Sleep, sleep, sleep, thou ti - ny child.
Sleep, sleep, sleep, thou ti - ny child.
Sleep, sleep, sleep, thou ti - ny child.
Thou - sand che - ru - bim, thou - sand ser - a - phim
Guard - ing o'er the bed of the great Lord of love.

France

WHAT IS THIS FRAGRANCE SO APPEALING?

(Quelle est cette odeur agréable?)

Traditional French Carol

1. What is this fra - grance so ap - peal - ing,
2. What is this star with bril - liance shin - ing
3. In Beth - le - hem, a sim - ple man - ger,
Shep - herds, that fills the wind - chilled air? Love - li - er
deep in the dark that blinds our sight? Nev - er did
is born to you a Sa - vior King. Hur - ry to
per - fume ne'er came steal - ing From the sweet blos - soms
morn - ing's sun come dawn - ing with a more ra - diant,
kneel be - side his man - ger your ar - dent praise and
of spring fair. What is this fra - grance so ap -
glo - rious light. What is this star with bril - liance
wor - ship bring. In Beth - le - hem, a sim - ple
peal - ling, shep - herds, that fills the wind - chilled air?
shin - ing deep in the dark that blinds our sight?
man - ger, is born to you a Sa - vior King.

France

TOURO-LOURO-LOURO

Traditional Provençal Carol

Nicolas Saboly, 1614-1675

1. Tou - ro - lou - ro - lou - ro, cocks are crow - ing, Long be -
2. Tou - ro - lou - ro - lou - ro, cold winds howl - ing, Make my
3. Tou - ro - lou - ro - lou - ro, what good for - tune, I have
fore the morn - ing light, High a - bove, the stars are
bod - y numb with cold, But I can - not yet be
found the Ho - ly Child! There u - pon the straw, the
shin - ing, O'er the Ho - ly Land to - night. "Will you go
stop - ping, For the day is grow - ing old. "Please let me
hand - some Ba - by looks at me and smiles! "Good day to
(p) (mf) (p)
there?" "No, I can - not!" "Go with me there?" "No, I can -
rest." "No rest for you." "I must find rest." "No rest for
you!" (He's laugh - ing now!) "Good day to you!" (Jo - seph's so

(mf) (p) (mf)
not." O Wil - liam, O Wil - liam, If I
you." O farm - er, O farm - er, Give me
proud!) O Ma - ry, O Ma - ry, May your
nev - er should re - turn, Say a psalm to give me bless -
shel - ter for the night, In the hay - loft I'd be sleep -
name be ev - er blessed, For the Child that Heav - en sent
ing! Still, I must go, Yea,
ing. Shel - ter, I do pray, Just,
thee! Saint Jo - seph too, Bless -
I must go; Through the jour - ney will be
for this day; For I'm near to freez - ing
ings un - to you! For the love - ly Child so
long, Still I must go, Yea, I must go.
now. Don't let me die! Don't let me die!
dear, That we all love, That we all love.

France

WHENCE COMES THIS RUSH OF WINGS AFAR?

(Noël des ausels)

Bas-Quercy Carol

1. Whence comes this rush of wings a - far, Fol - low - ing straight the
2. "Tell us, ye birds, why come ye here, In - to this sta - ble
3. Hark how the green finch bears his part, Phil - o - mel, too, with
4. An - gels and shep - herds, birds of the sky, Come where the Son of
No - el star? Birds from the woods in
poor and drear?" "Hast - 'ning we seek the
ten - der heart Chants from her leaf - y
God doth lie. Christ on earth with
won - drous flight, Beth - le - hem seek this ho - ly night.
new - born King, And all our sweet - est mu - sic bring.
dark re - treat, "Re mi fa sol" in ac - cents sweet.
man doth dwell, Join in the shout, "No - el, No - el."

Germany

A BABE IS BORN IN BETHLEHEM

(Ein Kind geborn zu Bethlehem)

Latin, 14 Century
Translated by Philip Schaff, 1869

Ludvig Lindeman, 1869

1. A Babe is born in Beth - le - hem, In Beth - le - hem; There - fore re - joice Je - ru - sa - lem. Al - le - lu - jah, al - le - lu - jah.
2. He doth with - in a man - ger lie, A man - ger lie; Whose throne is set a - bove the sky. Al - le - lu - jah, al - le - lu - jah.
3. The wise men came, led by the star, Led by the star; Gold, myrrh and in - cense, brought from far. Al - le - lu - jah, al - le - lu - jah.
4. On this most bless - ed Ju - bi - lee, Blest Ju - bi - lee; All glo - ry be, O God, to Thee. Al - le - lu - jah, al - le - lu - jah.

Germany

BESIDE THY CRADLE HERE I STAND

(Ich steh' an deiner Krippe hier)

Paul Gerhardt, 1607-1676
translated by J. Troutbeck, 1832-1899

Geistliche Gesangbuch
harmonized by Johann Sebastian Bach

Be - side Thy cra - dle here I stand, O
And bring Thee with a will - ing hand The
Thou that ev - er liv - est,
ver - y gifts Thou giv - est.
Ac - cept me, 'tis my mind and heart, My soul, my strength, my
ev - 'ry part That Thou from me de - sir - est.

Germany

BREAK FORTH, O BEAUTEOUS HEAVENLY LIGHT

(Brich un, du schönes Morgenlicht)

Johann Rist, 1641
translated by John Troutbeck

Johan Schop, 1641
harmonized by Johann Sebastian Bach

Break forth, O beau - teous heaven - ly light, and ush - er _ in the
morn - ing, You shep - herds, shud-der not with _ af - fright, but
hear the _ an - gel's warn - ing. This _ child, now weak _ in
in - fan - cy, our _ con - fi - dence _ and _ joy _ shall be, the
pow-er of Sa - tan _ break - ing, our _ peace e - ter - nal _ mak - ing.

Germany

FROM HEAVEN ABOVE

(Vom Himmel hoch)

Martin Luther, 1483-1546

V. Schumann, *Geistliche Lieder*, 1539

1. From heav'n a - bove to earth I come To
2. To you this night is born a child Of
3. This is the Christ, God's Son most high, Who
4. The bless - ing which the Fa - ther planned The
bring good news to ev - 'ry - one! Glad tid - ings of great
Mar - y, cho - sen vir - gin mild; This new - born child of
hears your sad and bit - ter cry; He will him - self your
Son holds in his in - fant hand, That in his king - dom,
joy I bring To all the world, and glad - ly sing:
low - ly birth Shall be the joy of all ___ the earth.
Sav - ior be And from all sin will set ___ you free.
bright and fair, You may with us his glo - ry share.

Germany

GOOD CHRISTIAN MEN, REJOICE

(In dulci jubilo)

Anonymous, 1300
translated by John M. Neale, 1853

14th Century German Melody

1. Good Chris - tian men, re - joice With heart and soul and voice,
2. Good Chris - tian men, re - joice With heart and soul and voice,
3. Good Chris - tian men, re - joice With heart and soul and voice,
Give ye heed to what we say: Je - sus Christ is
Now ye hear of end - less bliss: Je - sus Christ was
Now ye need not fear the grave: Je - sus Christ was
born to - day! Ox and ass be - fore Him bow, And He is in the
born for this. He hath ope'd the heav'n - ly door, And man is bless - ed
born to save. Calls you one and calls you all, To gain His ev - er -
man - ger now; Christ is born to - day! Christ is born to - day.
ev - er-more; Christ was born for this. Christ was born for this.
last - ing hall; Christ was born to save. Christ was born to save.

Germany

JOSEPH DEAREST, JOSEPH MINE

(Josef lieber, Josef mein)

Traditional German Text

14th Century German Melody

1. Jo - seph, dear - est Jo - seph mine, Help me cra - dle the Babe di - vine,
2. Glad - ly, Moth - er Ma - ry mine, Will I rock the Babe di - vine,
Sing to Him a lull - a - bye: 'Now sleep and rest, Your slum - ber blest, O
While I sing a lull - a - bye: 'O sleep and rest, Your slum - ber blest, O
Refrain
Je - sus!'
Je - sus!'
He came a - mong us at Christ - mas time, At Christ - mas time in
Beth - le - hem, Bring - ing all men far and wide Love's Di - a - dem.
Ei - a, ei - a. Je - sus Christ, who came to earth to save us.

Germany

LO, HOW A ROSE E'ER BLOOMING

(Es ist ein' Ros'entsprungen)

15th-Century German
translated by Theodore Baker, 1894

Alte Catholische Geistliche Kirchengesäng, 1599
harmonized by Michael Praetorius, 1609

1. Lo, how a Rose e'er bloom - ing from ten - der stem hath sprung! Of Jes - se's lin - eage com - ing, as men of old have sung. It came, a flower - et bright, a - mid the cold of win - ter, when half spent was the night.
2. I - sa - iah 'twas fore - told it, the Rose I have in mind; with Ma - ry we be - hold it, the Vir - gin Moth - er kind. To show God's love a - right, she bore to us a Sav - ior, when half spent was the night.

Germany

O CHRISTMAS TREE

(O Tannenbaum)

Traditional German Carol

1. O Christ - mas tree, O Christ - mas tree, How true your leaves un - chang - ing; Not on - ly green in sum - mer's heat, But al - so win - ter's snow and sleet, O Christ - mas tree, O Christ - mas tree, With faith - ful leaves un - chang - ing.
2. O Christ - mas tree, O Christ - mas tree, Of all the tress most love - ly; Each year, you bring to me de - light, ___ shin - ing in the Christ - mas night, O Christ - mas tree, O Christ - mas tree, Of all the trees most love - ly.
3. O Christ - mas tree, O Christ - mas tree, Your leaves will teach me, al - so, That hope and love and faith - ful - ness, Are sa - cred things I can pos - sess. O Christ - mas tree, O Christ - mas tree, Your leaves will teach me, al - so.

Germany

O COME, LITTLE CHILDREN

(Ihr Kinderlein, kommet)

C. von Schmidt, 1840

J.P.A. Schulz, 1840

1. O come, lit - tle chil - dren, O come one and all, To
2. He's born in a sta - ble for you and for me, Draw
3. See Ma - ry and Jo - seph with love beam - ing eyes Are
4. Kneel down and a - dore Him with shep - herds to - day, Lift
Beth - le - hem haste, to the man - ger so small, God's
near by the bright gleam - ing Star - light to see, In
gaz - ing up - on the rude bed where He lies, The
up lit - tle hands now and praise Him as they; Re -
Son for a gift has been sent you this night To
swad - dling clothes ly - ing so meek and so mild, And
shep - herds are kneel - ing, with hearts full of love, While
joice that a Sav - ior from sin you can boast, And
be ___ your re - deem - er, your joy ___ and de - light.
pur - er than an - gels the heav - en - ly child.
an - gels sing loud hal - le - lu - jahs a - bove.
join ___ in the song of the heav - en - ly host.

Germany

O THOU JOYFUL

(O du fröhliche)

John Falk, st. 1; st. 2 & 3 anon.
translated by H. Ketterjohn, 1919

Sicilian Melody, 1794

1. O thou joy - ful, O thou won - der-ful Grace re - veal - ing
2. O thou joy - ful, O thou won - der-ful Love re - veal - ing
3. O thou joy - ful, O thou won - der-ful Peace re - veal - ing
Christ - mas - tide! Je - sus came to win us From all sin with - in us:
Christ - mas - tide! Loud ho - san - as sing - ing And all prais - es bring - ing,
Christ - mas - tide! Dark - ness dis - ap-pear - eth, God's own light now near - eth,
Glo - ri - fy, glo - ri - fy the hol - ly child.
May thy love, may thy love with us a - bide.
Peace and joy, peace and joy to all be - tide.

Germany

RING, LITTLE BELLS

(Kling, Glöckchen)

Karl Enslin, 1814-1875

Traditional German Carol

Ring, bells, go ding - a - ling - a - ling, Ring, lit - tle bells!
1. O how cold the win - ter! Will you let Me en - ter?
2. Maid and In - fant ten - der, Will you let Us en - ter?
3. In our hearts now steal - ing, Hap - pi - ness the feel - ing,
Do not block the door - way On my bless - ed birth - day!
To us shel - ter giv - ing And the Child prais - ing?
Joy and bless - ing ho - ly From the Child so low - ly,
Ring, bells, go ding - a - ling - a - ling. Ring, lit - tle bells!

Germany

SUSANI

14th-Century German Carol

Melody from Cologne, 1623

1. From Heav - en on high, O an - gels sing!
2. Come bring your in - stru - ments so sweet!
3. O lift your voi - ces clear and high!
4. Sing Peace to all peo - ple far and wide!
Ei - a, ei - a! Su - sa - ni, su - sa - ni, su - sa - ni!
And let the joy - ful trum - pets ring!
With harp and chimes your Sa - vior greet!
With strings and or - gan raise the cry!
And praise to God, our heav'n - ly guide!
Al - le - lu - ia! Al - le - lu - ia! Of Mar - ry we sing, and Christ, her Son.

Germany

TO US IS BORN A LITTLE CHILD

(Ein Kindelein ist uns geboren)

Traditional Text

Köln Gesangbuch, 15th Century

1. To us is born a lit - tle Child Of Ma - ry, maid - en moth - er mild, Yule - time a mer - ry sea - son is, Babe Je - sus our de - light and bliss.
2. Strange sight with - in a sta - ble old, Lo! God is born in want and cold, O self - ish world, this Babe, I say, Doth put thee to the blush to - day.
3. Now an - gels joy - ful hymns up - raise, And God's own Son with car - ols praise. To Beth - le - hem the shep - herds fare, And first - lings of their flock they bear.
Refrain
O Je - sus dar - ling of my heart, How rich in mer - cy, Babe, Thou art.

Germany

WHILE BY MY SHEEP

(Als ich bei meinen Schaffen wacht)

Traditional Text

Trier Gesangbuch, 1871

1. While by my sheep I watched at night, Glad tid - ings brought an an - gel bright.
2. There shall be born, so he did say, In Beth - le - hem, a Child to - day.
3. There shall He lie, in man - ger mean, Who shall re - deem the world from sin.
4. Lord, ev - er - more to me be nigh, Then shall my heart be filled with joy!
Refrain
How great my joy, great my joy. Joy, joy, joy, Joy, joy, joy! Praise to the Lord in Heav'n on high. Praise to the Lord in Heav'n on high.
(p)
(f)

Ireland

IRISH CAROL

Traditional Irish Carol

1. Christ - mas Day is come; let's all pre - pare for mirth, Which
2. But why should we re - joice? Should we not ra - ther mourn, To
3. Oh! cease, ye bless - ed an - gels, such clam - 'rous joys to make! Though
4. If we would then re - joice, let's can - cel the old score, And,
fills the heav'ns and earth at this a - maz - ing birth. Through
see the hope of na - tions thus in a sta - ble born? Where
mid - night si - lence fa - vours, the shep - herds are a - wake; And
pur - pos - ing a - mend-ment, re - solve to sin no more; For
both the joy - ous an - gels in strife and hur - ry fly, With
are his crown and scep - tre, where is his throne sub - lime, Where
you, O glo - rious star! that with new splen - dor brings, From
mirth, can ne'er con - tent us, with - out a con - science clear; And
glor - ry and ho - san-nas, 'All Ho - ly' do they cry, In heav'n the church tri - um-phant a -
is his train ma - jes - tic that should the stars out-shine? Is there no sump-tuous pal - ace, nor
the re - mot - est parts three learn - ed east - ern kings, Turn some - where else your lus - tre, your
thus we'll find true pleas-ure in all the u - sual cheer, In danc - ing, sport - ing, re-v'ling with
dores with all her choirs, The mil - i - tant on earth, with hum - ble faith ad - mires
an - y inn at all, To lodge his heav'n-ly moth-er, but in a filth - y stall?
rags else-where dis - play, For Her-od may slay the Babe, and Christ must straight a - way.
mas - quer - ade and drum, So Christ - mas mer - ry be, as Chris-tians doth be - come

Ireland

LOVE CAME DOWN AT CHRISTMAS

Christina Rossetti

Melody from *Petrie Collection of Irish Melodies, Part II,* 1902

1. Love came down at Christ - mas, love all love - ly, love di - vine;
2. Wor - ship we the God - head, love in - car - nate, love di - vine;
3. Love shall be our to - ken; love be yours and love be mine,
love was born at Christ - mas; star and an - gels gave the sign.
wor - ship we our Je - sus, but where - with for sa - cred sign?
love to God and neigh - bor, love for plea and gift and sign.

Ireland

THE SNOW LAY ON THE GROUND

Traditional Irish-English Carol

1. The snow lay on the ground, The star shone bright, When
2. 'Twas Ma - ry, Vir - gin pure, Of ho - ly Anne, That
3. Saint Jo - seph, too, was by To tend the Child; To
Christ our Lord was born On Christ - mas night. Ve - ni - te a - do -
brought in - to this world the God made man. She laid Him in a
guard Him and pro - tect His Moth - er mild; The an - gels hov - ered
re - mus Do - mi - num; Ve - ni - te a - do - re - mus
stall At Beth - le - hem, The ass and ox - en share the
round, And sang this song: Ve - ni - te a - do - re - mus
Refrain
Do - mi - num.
night with them.
Do - mi - num.
Ve - ni - te a - do - re - mus
Do - mi - num, Ve - ni - te a - do - re - mus Do - mi - num.

Ireland

WEXFORD CAROL

Traditional Irish Carol

1. Good peo - ple _ all this Christ-mas time, Con - si - der well _ and
2. The night be - fore that hap - py tide, The no - ble Vir - gin
3. Near Beth - le - hem did shep-herds keep, Their flocks of lambs _ and
4. With thank - ful _ heart and joy - ful mind, The shep-herds went _ the
5. There were three _ wise men from a - far Di - rect - ed by _ a
bear in mind, What our good _ God for us has done, In
and her guide, Were long time _ seek - ing up and down, To
feed - ing sheep; To whom God's _ an - gels did ap - pear, Which
babe to find, And as God's _ an - gel had fore - told, They
glo - rious star, And on they _ wan - dered night and day, Un -
send - ing his _ be - lo - ved son. With Ma - ry ho - ly
find a lodg - ing in the town. But mark how all _ things
put the shep - herds in great fear. 'Pre - pare and go,' _ the
did our Sa - vior Christ be - hold. With - in a man - ger
til they came _ where Je - sus lay. And when they came _ un -
we should pray To _ God _ with love _ this Christ - mas Day; In
came to pass: From _ ev - 'ry door _ re - pell'd a - las! As
an - gels said, To _ Beth - le - hem, _ be not a - fraid; For
he was laid, And _ by _ his side _ the vir - gin maid, At -
to that place, Where _ our _ be - lov - ed Mes - si - ah was, They
Beth - le - hem, up - on that morn, There was a bless - ed Mes - si - ah born.
long fore - told, their re - fuge all, Was but an hum - ble ox - 's stall.
there you'll _ find, this hap - py morn, A prince - ly babe, _ sweet Je - sus born.
tend - ing _ on the Lord of life, Who came on earth _ to end all strife.
hum - bly _ cast them at his feet, With gifts of gold _ and in - cense sweet.

Italy

CAROL OF THE BAGPIPERS

(Canzone d'i zampognari)

Traditional Sicilian
translated by Theodore Baker, 1904

Traditional Sicilian

When Christ our Lord was born at Beth - le - hem a -
far, Al - though 'twas night, there shone as bright as noon, a
star. Nev - er so bright - ly nev - er so white - ly, Shone the
stars, as on that night! The bright - est star went A -
way to call the Wise Men from the O - ri - ent.

Italy

FROM STARRY SKIES THOU COMEST

(Tu scendi dalle stelle)

Alphonsus Liguori (1696-1787)

1. From star - ry skies Thou com - est, The King of Heav - en fore - told, Ap - pear - ing in a man - ger, Near fro - zen from the cold. Je - sus, pre - cious lit - tle Ba - by, How I long to make Thee warm! To shel - ter Thee from harm! My heart is filled with pi - ty, for Thy ti - ny form!
2. In Heav'n Thou wert Cre - a - tor, The True and On - ly Word, Yet here on earth no fire, Lord, To keep Thee from the cold. Je - sus, pre - cious lit - tle Ba - by, Come in strict - est pov - er - ty, Would I had gifts for Thee! How won - der - ful God's love that suf - fers here for me!

Italy

HARK! YE SHEPHERDS

Traditional Italian Carol

1. Hark! ye shep - herds, has - ten to the man - ger, Fear not to leave thy grazing sheep; Hear the host of heav - en loud pro - claim - ing, While God a - bove His watch doth keep. See now the light shin - ing a - bout thee, Sheer splen - dor glow - ing high and bright, It was fore - told by men ho - ly, ye would See Je - sus our dear Lord to - night.
2. Haste ye shep - herds, from the vale and moun - tain, This ho - ly night, this night di - vine, Thus spake an - gels, tell - ing the glad ti - dings, Of good - will, peace to all man - kind. Now fol - low quick - ly God's bright bea - con, Pro - tect - ing all who hur - ry past, Ba - by Je - sus waits thy hum - ble greet - ing And of - fer - ing of all thou hast.

Italy

JESUS, THE NEWBORN BABY

(Gesù bambin lé nato)

Traditional Italian Carol

1. Je - sus, the new - born Ba - by. Lies here in Beth - le -
2. We hear a gen - tle voice sing, Songs for the Ho - ly
hem; Born in a hum - ble man - ger
One, Jo - seph the Ba - by's fath - er
Is Heav - en's pre - cious Gem. He is a pre - cious
Nes - tles Him close and warm. "Sleep sweet - ly my dear
Gem, Al - though we find Him cry - ing! In Ma - ry's arms He's
Son." O see, him com - fort Je - sus, His ti - ny Ba - by
sigh - ing, Je - sus, our Di - a - dem.
sooth - ing! Glo - ry to God's own son!

Italy

MARY, DEAR MOTHER OF JESUS

Traditional Italian Carol

1. Ma - ry, dear moth - er of Je - sus, our Lord, We
2. Ma - ry, sweet moth - er of the ho - ly child, Born
haste to the crib with joy - ful ac - cord,
that all man - kind might be rec - on - cil'd,
To see God's own gift on this Christ - mas day,
Thy in - fant son was God - sent from a - bove,
Voic - ing our prais - es, The star lights our way.
All thanks be to Him, For this gift of love.

Italy

OH! DEAR JESUS

Traditional Italian Carol

1. Thou cam - est from heav'n we are ___ told, To keep God's pro - mise
2. Thy pil - grim - age through star - ry ___ skies, We greet with hos - an -
made of old, His will was re - deem'd at Thy ___ birth
nas loud rise! God's love made man - i - fest to ___ men,
Thus we all wel - come Thee to earth.
For God His on - ly Son hath giv'n.
Oh! dear Je - sus,
sweet an - gel - ic child, ___ Oh! dear Je - sus, pre - cious Sav - ior mine, ___
Oh! dear Je - sus, Oh! dear Je - sus, Keep my love, it is ev - er Thine.

Italy

OH! INFANT JESUS

Traditional Italian Carol

1. Oh! in - fant Je - sus, Thee I love; Kin - dle a flame
2. Oh! ho - ly in - fant, Thee I love; Be kind to all
with - in my breast, Let Thy spir - it di - vine dwell there - in So I
who dwell on earth, Child of grace, to Thee I hum - bly pray While I
will nev - er - more be dis - tress'd.
kneel and mar - vel at your birth.
With hearts that o - ver -
flow with love, We wor - ship Thee, King of Heav'n a - bove.

Italy

SLEEP, O SLEEP, MY PRECIOUS CHILD

(Dormi, dormi, o bel bambin)

Traditional Italian Carol

1. Sleep, o sleep, my pre - cious Child, King di - vine, King di - vine. Close Your eyes and sweet - ly slum - ber, King di - vine, King di - vine.
2. O my dar - ling, do not weep! Sweet - ly sleep, Sweet - ly sleep, Close Your eyes my Son, my dear one. Sweet - ly sleep, sweet - ly sleep.
(mf)
(p)
(mf)
Close Your eyes and sweet - ly slum - ber.
Close Your eyes, my Son, My dear one.
Refrain
Fa la la la, Fa la la la la, Fa la

la la, Fa la la la, Fa ___ la, ___
Fa ___ la, ___ Fa ___ la, ___ Fa ___ la.

Italy

OH! NIGHT AMONG THE THOUSANDS

Traditional Italian Carol

Oh! night a - mong the thou - sands, You are a won - drous
Oh! night a - mong the thou - sands, The night when Christ was
sight, Slow - ly the dark - ness fad - ed, A star shines high and
born, An - gels ac - claim your com - ing, The star gleams like the
bright. From _ whence comes this lu - mi - nous star? What is it the an - gels
dawn. Now _ hear the heav - en - ly voic - es Ex - ult as they loud - ly
sing?
sing:
It _ is the night of thou - sands the _ birth - day _ of our King!

Mexico

THE BABE

Traditional Mexican Lullaby Carol

Refrain
A la ru - ru - ru, My love - ly Je - sus, In sweet-est slum - ber now rest, my
dear - est.
Fine
1. You el - e - phant so huge, you small mos -
2. O night of glo - ry, night of ce - le -
3. Such heav'n - ly voi - ces in sweet ac - cents
D.C.
qui - to, Be ver - y still, you must not wake the Ba - by.
bra - tion, So rich - ly blest by Ma - ry, Queen of Heav - en.
sing - ing, The glo - rious tid - ings of His birth are ring - ing!

Mexico

PRAY, GIVE US LODGING

(En nombre del Cielo)

Traditional Mexican Carol

1. Joseph: Pray give us lod - ging dear, sir, in the name of Heav'n
2. Host: You can not stop here, I won't make my home an inn;
3. Joseph: Please show us pi - ty! Your heart can not be this cold!
4. Host: You try my pa - tience! I'm tired and must get some rest;
All day since morn - ing to tra - vel we're giv'n,
I do not trust you, your sto - ry is thin.
Look at poor Ma - ry, so worn and so tired!
I've told you kind - ly, but still you in - sist.
Ma - ry, my wife, is ex - pec - ting a child;
You two might rob me and then run a - way
We are most poor, but I'll pay what I can;
If you don't go and stop both - er - ing me,
She must have re - fuge to - night. Let us in! Let us in!
Find some - where else you can stay. Go a - way! Go a - way!
God will re - ward you good man! Let us in! Let us in!
I'll fix you, I gua - ran - tee! Go a - way! Go a - way!

Additional Lyrics

5. Joseph: Sir, I must tell you, my wife is the Queen of Heaven,
Chosen by God to deliver, his Son.
Jesus is coming to earth late this eve;
(O Heaven, make him believe!)
Let us in! Let us in!

6. Host: Joseph, dear Joseph! O how could I be so blind?
Not to know you and the Virgin so fine!
Enter, blest trav'lers, my house is your own;
Praise be to God on His throne!
Please come in! Please come in!

Netherlands

IN BETHLEHEM, THE LOWLY

Dutch Carol, 1638

1. In Beth - le - hem, the low - ly, Je - sus was born this
2. My heart in God re - joic - es, He is my Lord and
day, Him will I wor - ship on - ly, While on this earth I
King, And with a thous - and voi - es, My praise to Him I
stay. Oh! Yes! Oh! Yes! Je - sus was born this day.
sing. Oh! Yes! Oh! Yes! He is my Lord and King.

Netherlands

TODAY WE WELCOME A TINY CHILD

(Ons is geboren een kindekin)

Traditional 14th Century Dutch Carol

1. To - day we wel-come a ti - ny Child that pales the sun's bright shin - ing; Our
2. The stars that fill __ the ra - diant sky an - nounce the gift from Heav - en, While

hope __ and joy, this In - fant mild, whom an - gels songs are pro - claim - ing.
Ma - ry a - dores her Ho - ly Child, that God the Fa - ther has giv - en.

Norway

I AM SO GLAD ON CHRISTMAS EVE

(Jeg er saa glad hver julekveld)

Marie Wexelsen, 1832-1911

Peder Knudsen, 1819-1863

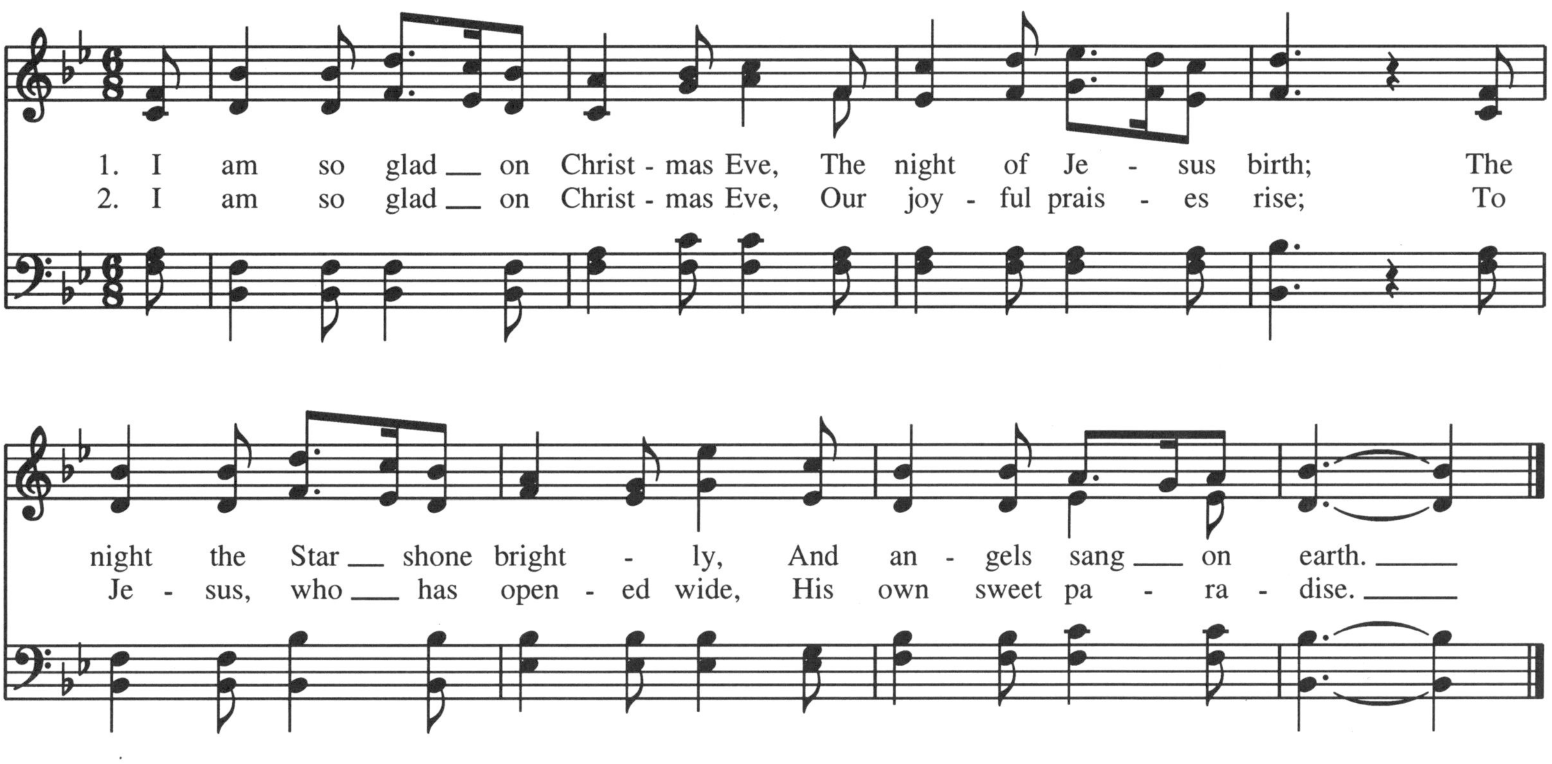
1. I am so glad __ on Christ - mas Eve, The night of Je - sus birth; The
2. I am so glad __ on Christ - mas Eve, Our joy - ful prais - es rise; To
night the Star __ shone bright - ly, And an - gels sang __ on earth. ____
Je - sus, who __ has open - ed wide, His own sweet pa - ra - dise. ____

Norway

O CHRISTMAS, YOU SEASON OF CHILDLIKE DELIGHT

(O jul med din glede)

Gustava Kielland

Traditional Norwegian Carol

1. O Christ-mas you sea-son of Child-like de-light, We all of-fer heart-i-est greet-ing; Our voi-ces we raise in a song clear and bright; To bid you a thous-and times wel-come.
2. O wise men who come from the lands of the East, We know of the Babe you are seek-ing; We pray we may join in your ho-ly quest, And fol-low the star bright-ly gleam-ing.
3. In joy and thanks-giv-ing I hold out my hand, And ask that you give yours in to-ken, That we be u-ni-ted by this sa-cred band; God's love through the a-ges un-bro-ken.
Refrain
Our hands we will clap, clap, clap, As hap-py as can be; So glad are we this day to see, We swing a-round a cir-cle and curt-sey.

Norway

YOU GREEN AND GLITTERING TREE

(Du grønne, glitrende tre)

Johan Krohn

C.E.F. Weyse

1. You green and glit - ter-ing tree ___ good-day! With joy and glad - ness we
2. When Je - sus came to the world ___ that day, The lar - gest star in the
3. Oft - times at eve - ning a - round ___ the hearth, Our dear - est Moth - er would
hail your com - ing, Be - decked with can - dles and span - gles gay, Your
sky He light - ed; He gave a bea - con to show the way, To
tell the sto - ry Of Je - sus love and his words di - vine, The
top - most star is as sun - light shin - ning! Our hearts' re - min - der, of
ev' - ry soul His sal - va - tion plight - ed. A - bove Him sing - ing, the
mem' - ry fills ___ our hearts ___ with glo - ry. The tree in splen - dor, our
Heav - en's splen - dor, Our hearts' re - min - der of Heav - en's splen - dor, And
an - gels wing - ing. A - bove him sing - ing, the an - gels wing - ing, O'er
hearts re - min - der, The tree in splen - dor, our hearts' re - min - der, Of
God's great love, and God's great love. ___
Beth - le - hem, o'er Beth - le - hem. ___
God's great love, of God's great love. ___

Poland

COME RUNNING, YOU SHEPHERDS

(O laufet, ihr Hirten)

Traditional Silesian Carol

1. Come run - ning, you shep - herds, as fast ___ as you can, With
2. This beau - ti - ful In - fant puts an - gels to shame! Be -
3. My friends ___ we're mak - ing a cra - dle for Him, To
flutes and with bag - pipes, and with ___ your whole clan. We're ___
side, Him, shy Jo - seph is whisp - er - ing His name. And ___
tuck Him in snug from the night ___ cold and grim. Loo ___
go - ing ___ to ___ see, In ___ Beth - le - hem's ___ stall, The
Ma - ry ___ is ___ there, So ___ sweet but ___ so ___ pale! My
loo, love - ly ___ Babe; loo ___ loo, go ___ to sleep. O
Child whom the an - gels pro - claimed ___ to us all.
heart fills with pi - ty to see ___ her so frail.
dear lit - tle Je - sus, loo, loo, ___ go to sleep.

Poland

INFANT HOLY, INFANT LOWLY

(W zlobie lezy)

Traditional Polish Carol

1. In - fant ho - ly, in - fant low - ly, for his
2. Flocks were sleep - ing, shep - herds keep - ing vig - il
bed a cat - tle stall; ox - en low - ing, lit - tle know - ing, Christ the
till the morn - ing new saw the glo - ry, heard the sto - ry tid - ings
babe is Lord of all. Swift are wing - ing an - gles sing - ing no - els
of a gos - pel true. Thus re - joic - ing, free from sor - row, prais - es
ring - ing, tid - ings bring - ing. Christ the babe is Lord of all.
voic - ing, greet the mor - row. Christ the babe was born to you.

Poland

LULLABY, JESUS

(Lulajze Jezuniu)

Traditional Polish Carol

1. Lull - a - by, Je - sus, O cease from your ___ cry - ing,
2. See how ___ God's earth lies in sor - row and ___ sad - ness;
Here on ___ Thy Moth - er's warm breast sweet - ly ly - ing.
Give us ___ Thy bless - ing, O bring Heav - en's glad - ness!
Refrain
Lull - a - by, ___ Je - sus, ___ O ___ sleep now, my pre - cious,
Moth - er ___ is watch - ing with love none can meas - ure.

Poland

O COME REJOICING

(Dzisaij w Bethlehem)

Traditional Polish Carol

1. O, come re - joic - ing, O, come re - joic - ing Beth - le - hem, re - joice ye!
2. Ma - ry is sing - ing, Ma - ry is sing - ing songs for Thee, dear Je - sus;
For of a Vir - gin, for of a Vir - gin God is born un - to thee!
Jo - seph is smil - ing, Jo - seph is smil - ing o'er the son so glo - rious
Refrain
Tru - ly He com - eth, Christ, our sal - va - tion, An - gels are sing - ing
Their ju - bi - la - tion; Shep - herds come to praise Him, Ox - en kneel be - fore Him,
What a Won - der God has giv'n.

Puerto Rico

IN BETHLEHEM'S CRADLE

(En el portal a Belén)

Traditional Puerto Rican Carol

1. He is born with - in a sta - ble, In the bit - ter cold of win - ter; 'Twixt the
2. There with - in the din - gy sta - ble, Sun and moon and star are shin - ing: Jo - seph,
3. To His side, a low - ly shep - herd, From the Span - ish fields ap - pear - ing, Brings the
4. Al - so near Him stands a gyp - sy, From Gra - na - da he comes hie - ing. Bring - ing
ox and ass He's ly - ing, Heav - en's Child, the world's re - deem - er.
Ma - ry and the Child, _ For whom all our hearts were pin - ing.
Ba - by gifts of lin - en, So a shirt He can be wear - ing.
to the Child a roos - ter; "Cock - a - doo - dle - doo," it's cry - ing.
Refrain
Sing now of Je - sus, of the dear ba - by, O what a glo - rious gift from a -
bove! He has our hearts and all of our love! He has our hearts and all of our
love! Le - rum, le - rum, le - rum, la! ¡Que vi - va!

Puerto Rico

SONG OF THE WISE MEN

(De tierra lejana venimos)

Traditional Puerto Rican Carol

1. From a far - off home the Sav - ior we come seek - ing,
2. Glow-ing gold I bring the new - born Child so ho - ly,
3. Frank-in-cense I bring the child of God's own choos - ing,
4. Bit - ter myrrh have I to give the ti - ny Je - sus,
Us - ing as our guide the star, so bright - ly beam - ing.
To - ken of His pow'r to reign a - bove in glo - ry.
To - ken of our praise to Heav - en ev - er ris - ing.
To - ken of the pain that He will bear to save us.
Refrain
Love-ly East - ern Star, that tells us of God's great love, Heav-en won-drous light O nev - er cease thy shin - ing!
Glo - ry in the High - est to the Son of Heav - en And up-on the earth be peace and love to men.
1.
2.

Puerto Rico

PASTORES A BELÉN

(Shepherds, to Bethlehem)

Traditional Puerto Rican Carol

The Lord on earth is here, ap - pear - ing as a Ba - by, He
lies in Beth - le - hem, the bles - sed Son of Ma - ry.
O come, O come, O shep - herds, run to see,
The Ho - ly Child, That brings us Heav - en's peace.
Come car - ry - ing some nuts and some hon - ey, Of - fer them to Je - sus to eat, Come
car - ry - ing some nuts and some hon - ey, Of - fer them to Je - sus to eat.

Has - ten, has - ten, haste to a - dore! Je - sus is born, the
Son of our great Lord, Je - sus our King, for - ev - er - more.

Romania

AT THE GATES OF HEAVEN ABOVE

(Sus în poarta raiului)

Traditional Romanian Carol

1. At the gates of Heav - en a - bove, Ap - ple trees white are
2. At the gates of Heav - en a - bove, Ma - ry the Moth - er
3. At the gates of Heav - en a - bove, Her tin - ny Child is
4. At the gates of Heav - en a - bove, "Hush, pre - cious Son, I've
bloom - ing sweet - ly, Bloom - ing for Christ, most pre - cious love.
mild is sit - ting, Hold - ing the Babe, her dear - est love.
weep - ing sad - ly, weep - ing is Christ, her dear - est love.
gifts to give you, Gifts for the Christ, my dear - est love."

Scotland

BALOO, LAMMY

17 Century Scottish Melody

1. This day to you is born a Child, Of
2. And now shall Ma - ry's lit - tle Babe, For
3. Sleep sound - ly, King Je - sus, and know no fear, Thy
Ma - ry meek, the Vir - gin mild; That bless - ed
ev - er be our Hope and Joy; E - ter - nal
sub - jects a - dor - ing, watch o - ver Thee here, God's an - gels and
Bairn so lov - ing and kind, Shall now sing
be His reign on earth, Re - joice, then all
shep - herds, and kine in their stall, And wise men and
prais - es both heart and mind;
peo - ple, for this ho - ly birth;
Vir - gin Thy guar - dians all;
Ba - loo, Lam - my.

Spain

A LA NANITA NANA

Traditional Spanish Melody

A la na-ni-ta na-na na-ni-ta, e-a na-ni-ta e-a, Sleep, sleep my dear-est Je-sus, May peace at-
tend_Thee, may peace at-tend_Thee. To the world lit-tle Sav-ior, New hope Thou art bring-ing
All the world, lit-tle Sav-ior, Thy prais-es sing-ing, God's an-gels float-ing o'er Thee
chant al-le-lu-ia. A-la na-ni-ta na-na, na-ni-ta e-a.

Spain

BELLS OVER BETHLEHEM

(Campana sobre campana)

Traditional Andalucian Carol

1. Bells o - ver Beth - le - hem peal - ing, God's sa - cred pres - ence re - veal - ing!
2. Shep - herds if you but will has - ten, Ma - ry, the most Bless - ed Vir - gin,
There in the man - ger is rest - ing Je - sus, the earth's rich - est bless - ing!
May grant that you may be keep - ing Watch o'er the dear ba - by sleep - ing!
Refrain
The
bells, the bells of Beth - le - hem Are ring - ing out the ti - dings, "Good will to all men!"
Leave your sheep and come, O shep - herds, pres - ents bring the Child so low - ly,
Bring some cheese and bring some wine For the Moth - er Ma - ry ho - ly. The
bells, the bells of Beth - le - hem Are ring - ing out the tid - dings, "Good will to all men!"

Spain

CAROL OF THE BIRDS

(El chant dels ocells)

Traditional Catalonian Carol

1. Up - on this won-d'rous night, When God's great star ap - pears, And floods the earth with bright - ness,
2. The Night - in - gale is first To bring his song of praise, And tell us of his glad - ness:
3. The an-sw'ring Spar - row cries: "God comes to earth this day A - mid the an - gels soar - ing."
4. The Par-tridge adds these words: "To Beth - le - hem I'll fly; Where in the stall He's ly - ing.
Birds' voi - ces rise in song, And, warb-ling all night long, Ex - press their glad hearts'
"Je - sus our Lord, is born, To free us from all sin, And ban - ish ev - 'ry
Trill - ing in sweet-est tones, The Finch his Lord now owns: "To Him be all thanks -
There, near the man - ger blest, I'll build my - self a nest, And sing my love un -
light - ness. Birds' voi - ces rise in song, And,
sad - ness! "Je - sus, our Lord, is born, To
giv - ing." Trill - ing in sweet - est tones, The
dy - ing. There, near the man - ger blest, I'll
warb-ling all night long, Ex - press their glad hearts' light - ness.
free us from all sin, And ban - ish ev - 'ry sad - ness.
Finch his Lord now owns: "To Him be all thanks - giv - ing."
build my - self a nest, And sing my love un - dy - ing."

Spain

COME, ALL YE CHILDREN

Traditional Castilian Melody, 17th Century

1. Come, all ye chil - dren, your voic - es raise on this morn, on this morn,
2. Wake, all ye chil - dren, your Sav - ior was born this night, born this night,
3. Rise, all ye chil - dren, a love - ly day is dawn - ing, is dawn - ing,
Bring the glad tid - ings to men that Je - sus was born, Oh! Re - joice!
Fol - low the star for its beam send forth a bright light, Oh! Hark - en!
Rouse from your slum - bers and greet this Christ - mas morn - ing, Oh! Laud God!
Sweet - ly pro - long what the an - gels pro - claim, Lift up your voic - es, ac -
An - gel - ic choirs tell in sweet words of love, How the dear God sent his
Sing loud, sing well, 'tis the day of Christ's birth; While mor-tals slept, He de -
cent their re - frains, Sing, for Christ's birth will bring peace and joy to the earth.
Son from a - bove, How Je - sus' birth will re - deem all men up-on earth.
scend - ed to earth; Come, let us sing, for we know that Christ is our King!

Spain

COMPANIONS ALL, SING LOUDLY

(Canten en voz alta mis compañieros)

Traditional Basque Carol

1. Com - pan - ions, all sing loud - ly In praise of ___ Ma - ry
2. Say, Ma - ry, of sal - va - tion, Who brought these ___ ti - dings
3. Be - liev - est thou the an - gel, O Ma - ry, ___ tell us
dear, Look up and bear each proud - ly, The day of days is
nigh, This news of ex - al - ta - tion, Whence comes it us a -
true, What an - swer gav'st thou Ga - briel Of joy for that ye
near. On high ___ 'twas told ___ this sto - ry, That Ma - ry but ___ a
nigh? The an - gel Ga - briel spake us, On en - ter - ing ___ this
knew? The Lord ___ of heav'n ___ be prais - ed Both now and ev - er -
maid, Should bear the King of Glo - ry, In low - li - ness ar - ray'd.
house, That God shall not for - sake ___ us, But ran - som, by His cross.
more, Let songs of joy be rais - ed, Come hith - er and a - dore.

Spain

A FIRE IS STARTED IN BETHLEHEM

(En Belén tocan a fuego)

Traditional Castilian Carol

1. Here in Beth - le - hem this eve - ning, Springs a might - y Flame from
2. In a cold and hum - ble sta - ble, Blooms a per - fect white car -
3. Wash-ing swad - dling clothes for Je - sus, Ma - ry by a stream is
Heav - en, Whom our self - ish-ness will be con - sum - ing, And through whom we are for -
na - tion, That be-comes a love-ly pur-ple Li - ly, Sac - ri - ficed for our re -
sing - ing. Spar-rows chirp to hear a joy-ful greet - ing, And the rip - pling brook is
Refrain
giv - en.
demp - tion.
laugh - ing
Flash - ing and splash - ing, the fish - es in the
Flash - ing and splash - ing, the fish - es in the
riv - er, Splash - ing and bow - ing to Christ from Heav - en com - ing;
wa - ter, Splash - ing and prais - ing the Light from Heav - en dawn - ing.

Spain

FUM, FUM, FUM

Traditional Catalonian Carol

1. On De - cem - ber twen - ty - five sing Fum, fum, fum!
2. Lit - tle birds fly from the for - est, Fum, fum, fum!
3. Ti - ny stars up in the heav - ens, Fum, fum, fum!
On De - cem - ber twen - ty - five sing Fum, fum, fum! For the
Lit - tle birds fly from the for - est, Fum, fum, fum! All your
Ti - ny stars up in the heav - ens, Fum, fum fum! If you
love of us is giv'n The ho - ly Child, Son of heav'n Of the
fledg - lings leave be - hind And seek the in - fant Sa - vior kind. Come, and
See the Ba - by cry, O, do not an - swer with a sigh! Rath - er
Vir - gin, Jo - seph's bride, To all the earth good will be - tid - ing, Fum, fum, fum!
build a dow - ny nest to warm the love - ly Ba - by bles - sed, Fum, fum, fum!
light - en up the sky With Heav - en's beams of ra - diant bright - ness, Fum, fum, fum!

Spain

THE ICY DECEMBER

(El desembre congelat)

Traditional Catalonian Carol

1. Cold De - cem - ber winds were calm In the month of snow - ing.
2. When the dark - ness fell that night, Bring - ing sweet re - pos - ing,
3. Now the month of May was here, Filled with God's own ra - diance;
As the world fell dark one night, Spring - time's Hope was grow - ing;
All the land was hid from sight, Sleep our eyes was clos - ing.
Now the snow - white Li - ly bloomed, Flow'r of sweet - est fra - grance.
Then one rose - tree blos - somed new, One sweet flow - er
Sud - den - ly, there came a gleam From the sky, the
To the peo - ple far and near Came a breath of
on it grew. On the tree once bare, Grew the Rose so fair, Ah, the Rose, ah, the
glo - rious beam Of a heav'n - ly star, Giv - ing light a - far, Ah, the star, ah, the
heav'n - ly cheer; O, the in - cense rare, Of the Li - ly there! Ah, the scent, ah, the
Rose, Ah the Rose tree bloom - ing, Sweet the air per - fum - ing.
star, Ah, the star - beam glow - ing, Bright - ness e - ver grow - ing!
scent Of the Li - ly bloom - ing, All the air per - fum - ing.

Spain

KING HEROD

(El Rei Herodes)

Traditional Catalonian Carol

1. One day Jo - seph, rest - ing, the Child by his
2. "O Jo - seph, dear hus - band, from here we must
3. A - stride of a don - key, they hur - ried a -
side, Heard shout - ing and tu - mult that e - vil be -
go, And where we are go - ing no mor - tal must
long, Their path - way was nar - row, and dan - ger was
tide: "The wretch - ed King Her - od has made a de -
know. A - cross the hot de - sert to E - gypt we'll
strong; God's an - gels, and birds, fly - ing down from the
cree, For sol - diers to kill ev - 'ry in - fant they see."
flee, For there, dear - est Je - sus pro - tect - ed will be."
sky, The Ba - by, and Jo - seph, and Ma - ry did fly.

Spain

THE SON OF MARY

(El noi de la Mare)

Traditional Catalonian Carol

1. What shall we give to the Son of the Vir - gin? What can we give that the
2. What shall we give the Be - lov - ed of Ma - ry? What can we give to her
3. What shall we do if the figs are not rip - ened? What shall we do if the
Child will en - joy? First, we shall give him a tray full of rais - ins,
won - der - ful Child? Rai - sins and o - lives and nut - meats and ho - ney,
Figs are still green? We shall not cry; if they're not ripe for Eas - ter,
Then we shall of - fer sweet figs to the Boy. First, we shall give Him a
Can - dy and figs and some cheese that is mild. Rai - sins and o - lives and
On a Palm Sun - day, ripe figs will be seen. We shall not fret; if they're
tray full of rai - sins, then we shall of - fer sweet figs to the Boy.
nut - meats and hon - ey, Can - dy and figs and some cheese that is mild.
not ripe for Eas - ter, On a Palm Sun - day, ripe figs will be seen.

Spain

YA VIENE LA VIEJA

(Come, My Dear Old Woman)

Traditional Spanish Carol

1. Come, my dear old wo - man, With a lit - tle
2. Kings of Or - ient rid - ing, Cross the san - dy
3. Kings of Or - ient rid - ing, Guid - ed by the
pre - sent, That you love so dear - ly.
de - sert, Bring - ing to the Chi - ld,
star - light, Bring - ing to the Chi - ld,
Refrain
Of - fer it to Je - sus.
Wine and cook - ies sweet.
Gifts of love to - night.
We're weav - ing a gar - ment of green lem - on
leaves, For sweet Vir - gin Ma - ry, the Moth - er of God!

Sweden

THE HAPPY CHRISTMAS COMES ONCE MORE

(Det Kimer Nu Til Julefest)

Nicolai F.S. Grundtvig, 1817
translated by C.P. Krauth

C. Balle, 1850

1. The hap - py Christ - mas comes once more, The heav'n - ly Guest is at the door. The bless - ed words the shep - herds thrill, The joy - ous ti - dings: Peace, good will.
2. To Da - vid's cit - y let us fly, Where an - gels sing be - neath the sky; Through plain and vil - lage pres - sing near, And news from God with shep - herds hear.
3. O wake our hearts, in glad - ness sing, And keep our Christ - mas with our King, Till liv - ing song, from lov - ing souls, Like sound of might - y wa - ter rolls!

Sweden

YULETIDE IS HERE AGAIN

(Nu är det Jul igen)

Traditional Swedish Dance Carol

Yule - tide is here a - gain, the yule - tide is here a - gain, Let's
cel - e-brate, re - joice 'till Eas - ter.
1. Then when it's eas - ter - time, Yes
2. Ev - 'ry-one knows this real - ly
then, when it's Eas - ter - time, We'll cel - e-brate, re - joice 'till Christ - mas.
can - not be so, Be - cause of Lent, when we all must start fast - ing.

United States of America

AWAY IN A MANGER

unknown author vs. 1 and 2
John Thomas McFarland vs. 3

James R. Murray, 1887

1. A - way in a man - ger, No crib for a bed, The lit - tle Lord
2. The cat - tle are low - ing, The poor Ba - by wakes, But lit - tle Lord
3. Be near me, Lord Je - sus, I ask Thee to stay Close by me for -
Je - sus Laid down His sweet head, The star in the sky Looked
Je - sus No cry - ing He makes, I love Thee Lord Je - sus Look
ev - er, And love me, I pray. Bless all the dear chil - dren In
down where He lay, The lit - tle Lord Je - sus A - sleep on the hay.
down from the sky, And stay by my cra - dle Till morn - ing is nigh.
Thy ten - der care, And take us to heav - en, to live with Thee there.

* *This American carol was at one time erroneously attributed to Martin Luther, who wrote neither the text nor the music.*

United States of America

EVERYWHERE, EVERYWHERE, CHRISTMAS TONIGHT

Phillips Brooks (1835-1893)

Lewis H. Redner (1831-1908)

1. Christ - mas in lands of the fir - tree and pine, Christ - mas in
2. Christ - mas where chil - dren are hope - ful and gay, Christ - mas where
lands of the palm tree and vine, Christ - mas where snow - peaks stand
old men are pa - tient and gray, Christ - mas where peace like a
sol - emn and white: Christ - mas where corn - fields lie sun - ny and
dove in its flight Broods o'er brave men in the thick of the
bright. Ev - 'ry - where, ev - 'ry - where, Christ - mas to - night.
fight. Ev - 'ry - where, ev - 'ry - where, Christ - mas to - night.

United States of America

GATHER AROUND THE CHRISTMAS TREE

John H. Hopkins

Gath - er a-round the Christ - mas tree! Gath - er a-round the Christ - mas tree!
1. Ev - er - green have its branch - es been, It is king of all the wood - land scene; For
2. Once the pride of the moun - tain side, Now cut down to grace our Chirst - mas - tide: For
3. Ev - 'ry bough has a bur - den now, They are gifts of love for us, we trow. For
Chorus
Christ, our King, is born to - day! His reign shall nev - er pass a - way.
Christ from heav'n to earth came down, To gain, through death, a no - bler crown.
Christ is born, His love to show, And give good gifts to men be - low.
Ho - san - na, Ho - san - na, Ho - san - na in the high - est!

United States of America

GLAD CHRISTMAS BELLS

Anonymous American Carol

1. Glad Christ-mas bells, your mu - sic tells The sweet and pleas - ant
2. No pal - ace hall its ceil - ing tall His king - ly hand spread
3. Nor rai - ment gay, as there He lay, A - dorn'd the in - fant
4. But from a - far, a splen - did star The wise men west - ward
sto - ry; How come to earth, in low - ly birth, The Lord of life and glo - ry.
o - ver; There on - ly stood a sta - ble rude The heav'n - ly Babe to co - ver.
stan - ger; Poor, hum - ble child of moth - er mild She laid Him in a man - ger.
turn - ing; The live-long night saw pure and bright, A - bove His birth-place burn - ing.

United States of America

GO, TELL IT ON THE MOUNTAIN

African-American Spiritual

Refrain
Go, tell it on the moun - tain, O - ver the hills and
ev - 'ry - where; Go, tell it on the moun - tain That
Jesus Christ is born.
Fine
1. While shep-herds kept their watch-ing O'er si - lent flocks by night, Be - held through-out the heav - ens There shone a ho - ly light.
2. The shep-herds feared and trem-bled When lo! a - bove the earth Rang out the an - gel cho - rus That hailed our Sav - ior's birth.
3. Down in a low - ly man - ger The hum - ble Christ was born, And God sent us sal - va - tion That bless - ed Christ-mas morn.
D.C.

United States of America

I HEARD THE BELLS ON CHRISTMAS DAY

Henry W. Longfellow, 1863

John Baptiste Calkin, 1872

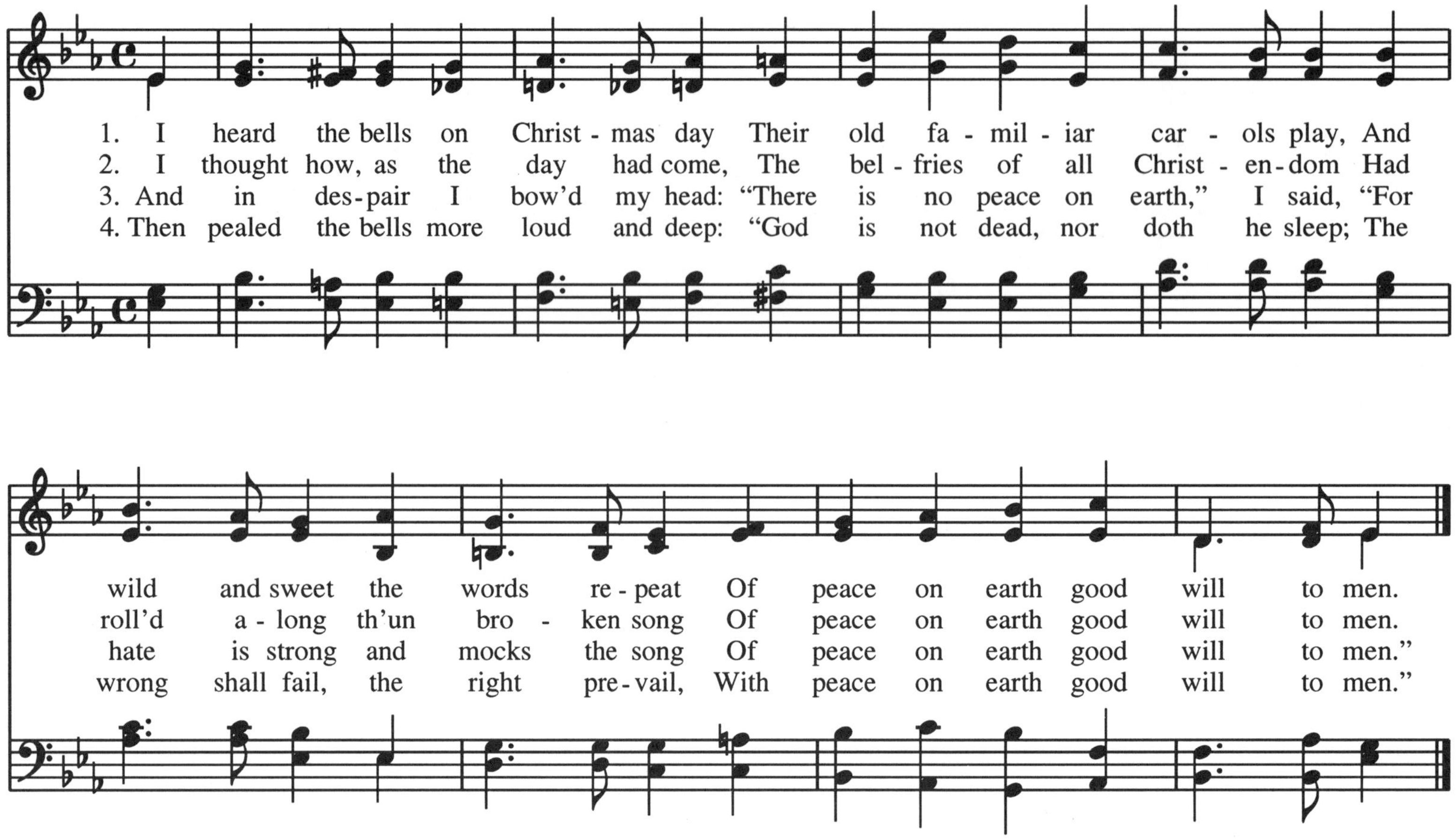
1. I heard the bells on Christ - mas day Their old fa - mil - iar car - ols play, And
2. I thought how, as the day had come, The bel - fries of all Christ - en - dom Had
3. And in des - pair I bow'd my head: "There is no peace on earth," I said, "For
4. Then pealed the bells more loud and deep: "God is not dead, nor doth he sleep; The
wild and sweet the words re - peat Of peace on earth good will to men.
roll'd a - long th'un bro - ken song Of peace on earth good will to men.
hate is strong and mocks the song Of peace on earth good will to men."
wrong shall fail, the right pre - vail, With peace on earth good will to men."

United States of America

IT CAME UPON THE MIDNIGHT CLEAR

Edmund H. Sears, 1849

Richard Storrs Willis, 1850

1. It came up - on the mid - night clear, that glo - ri - ous song of old, from
2. Still through the clo - ven skies they came with peace - ful wings un - furled, and
3. And ye, be - neath life's crush - ing load, whose forms are bend - ing low, who
4. For lo! the days are has - tening on, by proph - et seen of old, when
an - gels bend - ing near the earth, to touch their harps of gold: "Peace
still their heav - en - ly mu - sic floats o'er all the wea - ry world; a -
toil a - long the climb - ing way with pain - ful steps and slow, look
with the ev - er - cir - cling years shall come the time fore - told when
on the earth, good will to men, from hea-ven's all - gra - cious King." The
bove its sad and low - ly plains, they bend on hov - er - ing wing, and
now! for glad and gold - en hours come swift - ly on the wing. O
peace shall o - ver all the earth its an - cient splen - dors fling, and
world in sol - emn still - ness lay, to hear the an - gels sing.
ev - er o'er its Ba - bel sounds the bless - ed an - gels sing.
rest be - side the wea - ry road, and hear the an - gels sing!
the whole world send back the song which now the an - gels sing.

United States of America

JINGLE BELLS

James Pierpont, 1857

1. Dash-ing thro' the snow In a one horse o - pen sleigh, O'er the fields we go
2. Day or two a - go I thought I'd take a ride, And soon Miss Fan - nie Bright Was
3. Now the ground is white, Go it while you're young; Take the girls to - night, And
Laugh-ing all the way; Bells on bob - tail ring, Mak - ing spir - its bright; What
seat - ed by my side. The horse was lean and lank, Mis - for - tune was his lot, He
sing this sleigh-ing song; Just get a bob-tailed nag, Two for - ty for his speed, Then
fun it is to ride and sing A sleigh - ing song to - night!
got in - to a drift - ed bank, And we, we got up - sot.
hitch him to an o - pen sleigh, And crack! you'll take the lead.
Refrain
Jin - gle Bells! Jin - gle Bells!
Jin-gle all the way! Oh, what fun it is to ride In a one-horse o-pen sleigh!
1
2
one-horse o-pen sleigh!

United States of America

JOLLY OLD SAINT NICHOLAS

Anonymous, 19th Century American

1. Jol - ly old Saint Ni - cho - las, Lean your ear this way! Don't you tell a
2. When the clock is strik - ing twelve, When I'm fast a - sleep, Down the chim - ney
3. John - ny wants a pair of skates; Su - sy wants a sled; Nel - lie wants a
sin - gle soul what I'm going to say; Christ - mas Eve is com - ing soon;
broad and black, With your pack you'll creep; All the stock - ings you will find
pic - ture book; Yel - low, blue and red; Now I think I'll leave to you
Now, you dear old man, Whis - per what you'll bring to me; Tell me if you can.
Hang - ing in a row; Mine will be the short - est one, You'll be sure to know.
What to give the rest; Choose for me, dear San - ta Claus, You will know the best.

United States of America

MARY HAD A BABY

African-American Spiritual

Ma - ry had a ba - by, my Lord, Ma - ry had a ba - by, my Lord,
What did __ she call him, my Lord, What did __ she call him, my Lord,
Called him King _ Je - sus, my Lord, Called him King _ Je - sus my Lord,
Ma- ry had a ba - by, Ma - ry had a ba - by, Ma- ry had a ba - by, my Lord.
Ma- ry had a ba - by, Ma - ry had a ba - by, Ma- ry had a ba - by, my Lord.
Ma- ry had a ba - by, Called him King _ Je - sus. Ma- ry had a ba - by, my Lord.

United States of America

O LITTLE TOWN OF BETHLEHEM

Phillips Brooks, c. 1868

Lewis Redner, 1868

1. O lit - tle town of Beth - le - hem, how still we see thee
2. For Christ is born of Ma - ry, and gath - ered all a -
3. How si - lent - ly, how si - lent - ly, the won - drous gift is
4. O ho - ly Child of Beth - le - hem, de - scend to us we
lie; a - bove thy deep and dream - less sleep the si - lent stars go
bove, while mor - tals sleep, the an - gels keep their watch of won - dering
given; so God im - parts to hu - man hearts the bless - ings of his
pray; cast out our sin and en - ter in, be born in us to -
by. Yet in the dark streets shin - eth the ev - er - last - ing light; the
love. O morn - ing stars to - geth - er, pro - claim the ho - ly birth, and
heaven. No ear may hear his com - ing, but in this world of sin, where
day. We hear the Christ - mas an - gels the great glad ti - dings tell; O
hopes and fears of all the years are met in thee to - night.
prai - ses sing to God the King, and peace to all on earth!
meek souls will re - ceive him, still the dear Christ en - ters in.
come to us, a - bide with us, our Lord Em - man - u - el!

United States of America

RISE UP SHEPHERD AND FOLLOW

African-American Spiritual

(unison)
(parts)
(unison)
1. There's a star in the east on Christ-mas morn,
2. If you take good _ heed to the an - gel's word,
Rise up, shep-herd, and fol-low.
It will
You'll for -
(parts)
lead to the place where the Sa - vior's born, ___
get all your flocks, you'll for - get your herd, ___
Rise up, shep-herd, and fol - low. ___
Refrain
Leave your ewes and leave your lambs, Rise up, shep-herd and fol-low, ___ Leave your sheep and
leave your rams, Rise up, shep-herd and fol-low. __ Fol - low, fol - low, Rise up, shep-herd and
fol-low. ___ Fol-low the star of Beth - le - hem, ___ Rise up, shep-herd, and fol-low. ___

United States of America

THERE'S A SONG IN THE AIR

Josiah G. Holland, 1874

Karl P. Harrington, 1904

1. There's a song in the air! There's a star in the
2. There's a tu - mult of joy o'er the won - der - ful
3. In the light of that star lie the a - ges im -
4. We re - joice in the light, and we ech - o the
sky! There's a moth - er's deep prayer and a ba - by's low
birth, for the vir - gin's sweet boy is the Lord of the
pearled; and that song from a - far has swept o - ver the
song that comes down through the night from the heav - en - ly
cry! And the star rains its fire while the beau - ti - ful
earth. Ay! the star rains its fire while the beau - ti - ful
world. Ev - 'ry hearth is a - flame, and the beau - ti - ful
throng. Ay! we shout to the love - ly e - van - gel they
sing, for the man - ger of Beth - le - hem cra - dles a King!
sing, for the man - ger of Beth - le - hem cra - dles a King!
sing in the homes of the na - tions that Je - sus is King!
bring, and we greet in his cra - dle our Sav - ior and King!

United States of America

UP ON THE HOUSETOP

B.R. Handy

1. Up on the house - top the rein - deer pause, Out jumps good old San - ta Claus;
2. First, comes the stock - ing of lit - tle Nell; Oh, dear San - ta fill it well;
3. Next, comes the stock - ing of lit - tle Will; Oh, just see what a glo - rious fill!
Down thro' the chim - ney with lots of toys, All for the lit - tle ones, Christ - mas joys.
Give her a dol - lie that laughs and cries One that will o - pen and shut her eyes.
Here is a ham - mer and lots of tacks, Al - so a ball and a whip that cracks.
Ho, ho, ho! who would-n't go! Ho, ho ho! who would-n't go!
Up on the house - top click, click, click, Down thro' the chim-ney with good Saint Nick.

United States of America

WE THREE KINGS OF ORIENT ARE

John H. Hopkins, 1857

1. We three Kings of O - ri - ent are; Bear - ing gifts, we trav - erse a - far Field and foun - tain, moor and moun - tain, Fol - low - ing yon - der star.
2. Born a King on Beth - le - hem plain, Gold I bring, to crown Him a - gain, King for - ev - er ceas - ing nev - er O - ver us all to reign.
3. Frank - in - cense to of - fer have I, In - cense owns a De - i - ty nigh. Pray'r and prais - ing all men rais - ing, Wor - ship Him, God most high.
4. Myrrh is mine, its bit - ter per - fume Breathes a life of gath - er - ing gloom; Sor - r'wing, sigh - ing, bleed - ing, dy - ing, Sealed in the stone - cold tomb.
5. Glo - rious now be - hold Him a - rise, King and God and Sac - ri - fice, Al - le - lu - ia, Al - le - lu - ia, Earth to the heav'ns re - plies.
Chorus
O ___ Star of won - der, Star of night, Star with roy - al beau - ty bright, West - ward lead - ing, still pro - ceed - ing, Guide us to the per - fect light.

United States of America

WINDS THROUGH THE OLIVE TREES

Anonymous, 19th Century American

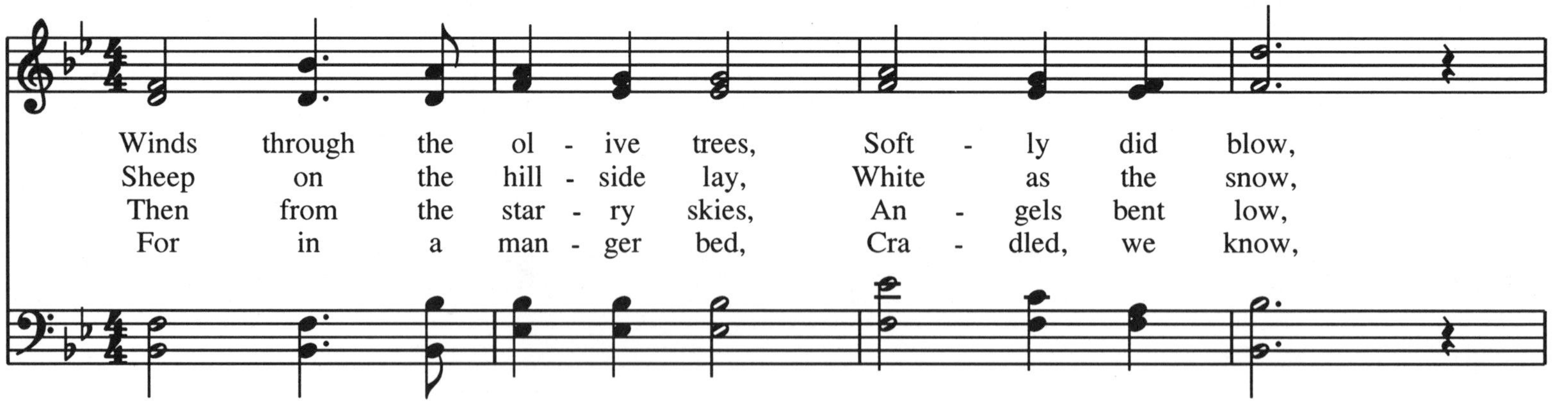
Winds through the ol - ive trees, Soft - ly did blow,
Sheep on the hill - side lay, White as the snow,
Then from the star - ry skies, An - gels bent low,
For in a man - ger bed, Cra - dled, we know,

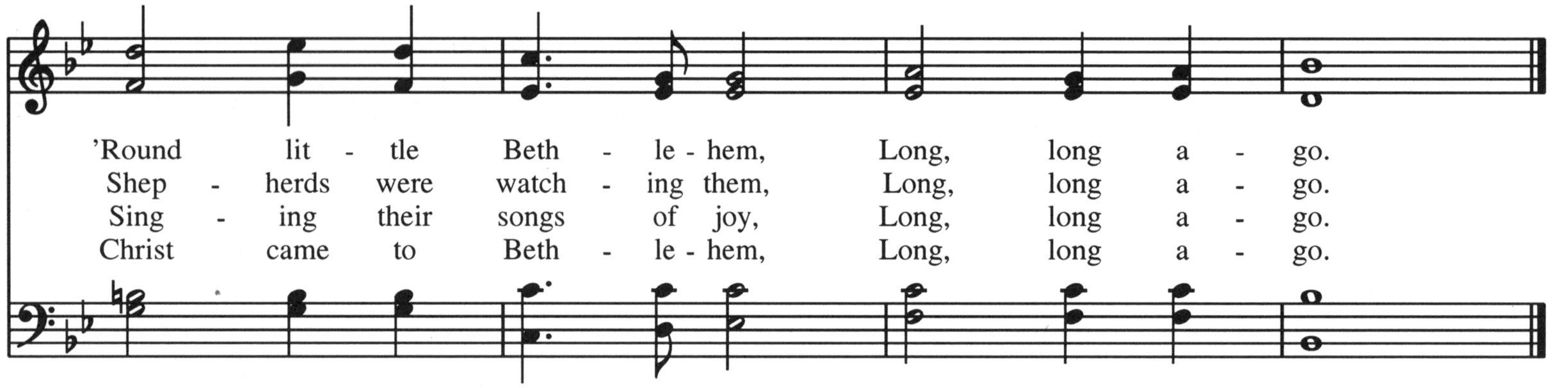
'Round lit - tle Beth - le - hem, Long, long a - go.
Shep - herds were watch - ing them, Long, long a - go.
Sing - ing their songs of joy, Long, long a - go.
Christ came to Beth - le - hem, Long, long a - go.

Venezuela

AS THE FRIGHTENED BABY JESUS

(Como busca el tierno infante)

Traditional Venezuelan Carol

As the fright - ened ba - by, Je - sus, Shiv - 'ring from the cold and
hun - ger. Sought re - pose and con - so - la - tion On the Vir - gin Moth - er's
breast; So would I, as dawn ap - proach - eth, Come to Thee, O Ho - ly
Ma - ry, Seek - ing Thy blest con - so - la - tion, And to pray for heav'n - ly rest.

Venezuela

WE ARE SINGING

(Cantemos)

Traditional Venezuelan Folk Carol

Refrain
Sing-ing, we are sing - ing Lov-ing praise we bring: Mer-ry Eve of
Christ - mas, Mer-ry Eve of Christ - mas, Mer-ry Eve of Christ - mas.
To Thee, In - fant King.
Fine
1. All our ex - pec - ta - tion, All our char - i - ty, All our con - so - la - tion, Child dear in Thee.
2. Beam-ing through the dark - ness, Flood-ing rays so bright, Shin-ing on the cra - dle, On the glo - rious night.
3. Night of cel - e - bra - tion, Night of Je - sus' birth, Night of ho - ly splen - dor, And re - deem - ing love.
D.C.
(Refrain after each Verse)

Wales

DECK THE HALL

Traditional Welsh Carol

1. Deck the hall with boughs of hol - ly, Fa la la la la, la la la la.
2. See the blaz - ing Yule be - fore us, Fa la la la la, la la la la.
3. Fast a - way the old year pass - es, Fa la la la la, la la la la.
'Tis the sea - son to be jol - ly, Fa la la la la, la la la la.
Strike the harp and join the cho - rus, Fa la la la la, la la la la.
Hail the new, ye lads and lass - es, Fa la la la la, la la la la.
Don we now our gay ap - pa - rel, Fa la la la la la la,
Fol - low me in mer - ry mea - sure, Fa la la la la la la,
Sing we joy - ous all to - geth - er, Fa la la la la la la,
Troll the an - cient Yule - tide car - ol, Fa la la la la, la la la la.
While I tell of Yule - tide treas - ures, Fa la la la la, la la la la.
Heed - less of the wind and weath - er, Fa la la la la, la la la la.

Wales

WELSH CAROL

Pastor K.E. Roberts

Traditional Welsh Caro

1. A - wake were they on - ly, those shep-herds so lone - ly, On guard in that si - lence pro -
2. May light new en - fold us, O Lord, for be - hold us Like shep-herds, from tu - mult with -
found, When co - lor had fa - ded, when night-time had sha - ded, Their sen - ses from sight
drawn, Nor heav-ing, nor see - ing, all oth - er care flee - ing, We wait the in - eff -
and from sound. Lo, Then broke a won - der, Then drif - ted a - sun -
a - ble dawn. O Spi - rit all - know - ing, Thou source o - ver - flow -
der The veils from the splen - dor of God, When light from the Ho - ly, came
ing, O move in the dark - ness a - round, That sight may be in us, true
down to the low - ly, And heav'n to the earth that they trod. Lo, trod.
hear - ing to win us, Glad ti - dings where Christ may be found. O found.
1
2